A Marriage Made for Heaven

A MARRIAGE MADE FOR HEAVEN

THE SECRETS OF HEAVENLY COUPLEHOOD

Couple Workbook

**Gregory K. Popcak, M.S.W., Ph.D.,
and Lisa A. Popcak**

A Crossroad Book
The Crossroad Publishing Company
New York

The Crossroad Publishing Company
www.CrossroadPublishing.com.

In continuation of our 200-year tradition of independent publishing, the Crossroad Publishing Company proudly offers a variety of books with strong, original voices and diverse perspectives. The viewpoints expressed in our books are not necessarily those of the Crossroad Publishing Company, any of its imprints, or of its employees. No claims are made or responsibility assumed for any health or other benefit.

Printed in the United States of America.

The text of this book is set in 11/15 Sabon. The display face is Triplex.

Cataloging-in-Publication Data is available from the Library of Congress
ISBN-10 0-8245-2532-9 (Leader Guide)
ISBN-13 978-0-8245-2532-3 (Leader Guide)
ISBN-10 0-8245-2533-7 (Couple Workbook) ISBN-13 978-0-8245-2533-0 (Couple Workbook)

1   2   3   4   5   6   7   8   9   10   14   13   12   11   10   09

CONTENTS

Heavenly Date Night #1 / Introduction
The Heavenly Purpose of Marriage 7

Heavenly Date Night #2
Your Heavenly Mission from God 15
       The Marital Imperative Exercise / 19

Heavenly Date Night #3 / Heavenly Communication
Plugging In to the Power of Grace 23

Heavenly Date Night #4 / Heavenly Rapport
Winning the Battle of the Sexes 33
       Heavenly Rapport Exercise / 39
       Help! I Feel Like I'm Losing Myself / 42

Heavenly Date Night #5 / Heavenly Love
Supercharging Friendship and Intimacy 47
       Lovestyle Quiz / 52

Heavenly Date Night #6 / Heavenly Problem Solving
Getting Out of Your Own Way 57
       Emotional Temperature Scale Exercise / 62

Heavenly Date Night #7 / Heavenly Gratitude
Never Feel Taken for Granted 67

Heavenly Date Night #8 / Heavenly Joy
Celebrating Life and Love Together 75

Heavenly Date Night #9 / Heavenly Fidelity
Getting Your Priorities in Order 83
       Heavenly Fidelity Exercise / 88

Heavenly Date Night #10 / Heavenly Family
Life and Love after Kids 93
       Lovelist Exercise / 98
       Marital Examination of Conscience / 99

Heavenly Date Night #11 / Heavenly Sex
The Secrets of Soulful Loving 103

Heavenly Date Night #12 / Heavenly Couplehood
Witnessing to the Power of Love 113

Heavenly Home Improvement Plan 117

Resource Guide 119

Contents

INTRODUCTION

The Heavenly Purpose of Marriage

OPENING THE SESSION

Summary of Session One

This session asserts that every married couple has been called and joined together by God primarily to do three things: (a) to be a witness to Christ's love for the church, (b) to help each other become the people God created them to be, and (c) to prepare each other to be happy with God in heaven. This session helps couples understand that through marriage they are for each other a physical sign of God's love. It also describes the outline for the coming year.

This first meeting concludes with a blessing by the pastor and a simple ceremony in which couples commit to becoming a Heavenly Couple. At the end of the year, those who complete the program will renew their vows and "earn their wings," pinning each other with a Heavenly Couple pin that was blessed during the ceremony.

Opening Prayer

Leader: Let's begin in the name of the Father and of the Son and of the Holy Spirit.

All: Amen.

Leader: Lord Jesus Christ, you are the author and source of all love. We come before you today to thank you for the gift of marriage and to commit ourselves both to discovering your plan for marriage and living out our vocation more fully. Open our hearts and minds to the wisdom of the Holy Spirit through the teaching of your church. Help each husband and wife gathered here today to become living witnesses to your love for each other.

Let's take a moment to offer the prayers of our hearts to the Lord. We'll all pray together, "Lord, teach us your love."

Petition 1:	For all the couples here today, that we would learn how to love one another as you love us. We pray to the Lord.
All:	Lord, teach us your love.
Petition 2:	Help us to remember that our first and most important task in marriage is to help each other get to heaven.
All:	Lord, teach us your love.
Petition 3:	Lord, help us to remember that you are our "First Spouse" and that all things in our relationship should come under your headship.
All:	Lord, teach us your love.
Leader:	If anyone would like to offer a petition of your own, please speak up now. (*Pause for petitions.*)
Leader:	Lord, we give you our hearts, minds, and strength. Teach us to love and serve one another and prepare each other to arrive, properly attired, at the Heavenly Wedding Feast. We entrust our prayers to the intercession of your mother as we pray,
All:	Hail Mary ... *Amen.*

❦❦ VIDEO AND DISCUSSION

Question #1: What are the most important reasons God has called you and your spouse together?

Question #2: What does it mean to say that "marriage is a sacrament"?

Question #3: What do the answers to the previous questions have to do with the everyday life of your marriage?

1

✿✿ COMMITMENT CEREMONY

Celebrant: A Reading of the Gospel According to St. John.
John 15:9–17

Celebrant: (*Join hands and face one another.*) Lord, these couples have chosen to commit themselves to learning how to love you more perfectly by living their marriage vows more fully. Bless them as they seek to apply your wisdom to the joys, struggles, and challenges of daily life. We ask this through Christ our Lord.

All: Amen.

Celebrant: God has given us married love as a sacred sign of his love for the world. Let us call upon the Author of Love, that he might instruct our hearts to live in his perfect love for one another.

Reader or Celebrant:
Please respond by praying, "Lord, renew our commitment to love."

That the Marriage Made for Heaven Program would bear abundant fruit in the hearts of the couples gathered here and in the hearts of those couples around the world who are likewise seeking to live the fullness of God's plan for marriage.

All: Lord, renew our commitment to love.

Reader or Celebrant:
That the couples gathered here would faithfully attend the sessions of the Marriage Made for Heaven Program and faithfully apply what they learn.

All: Lord, renew our commitment to love.

Reader or Celebrant:
That you would deliver the couples gathered here, and all married couples throughout the world, from the spirits of dissension, hostility, hopelessness, and divorce.

All: Lord, renew our commitment to love.

Reader or Celebrant:

That you would strengthen these couples here today, that they might learn to love each other with your love and live lives of generous, abundant, and joyful service to one another.

All: Lord, renew our commitment to love.

Reader or Celebrant:

That the couples gathered here would always remember that the most important work of their marriage is to help each other become the people you created them to be and to help each other arrive properly attired for the Eternal Wedding Feast.

All: Lord, renew our commitment to love.

Celebrant: O God, hear our prayers, and grant each of the couples gathered here the grace to imitate the Holy Family, that they might praise you and bear witness to your glory by living the fullness of your plan for marriage. We ask this through Christ our Lord.

All: Amen.

Celebrant: I would ask the couples to join hands, bow your heads, and pray for God's blessing:

Blessed are you, O Lord our God, King of the Universe. In the beginning, it pleased you to create man and woman and to invite them to share in celebrating and revealing the power of your love to the world.

✛ Bless these couples gathered here today. Look with kindness and mercy upon them as they strive to live the fullness of married love. May they be a beacon of light in a dark world that is hungry for the witness of godly love. Strengthen them through difficult times, grant them many joys, sustain the covenant of love between them through all their days, and give them many happy, grace-filled years together, surrounded by the blessed presence of their children and their children's children. We ask this through Christ our Lord.

All: Amen.

Name of couple we will pray for: _____

❧❧ ACTIVITY

Heavenly Home Improvement Plan

1. In order to know what God wants, we have to be committed to talking with him both individually and together every day. We'll talk more about couple prayer in a future meeting, but for now, we would invite you to commit to spending at least five minutes a day praying individually to know how God wants you to love your spouse that day, *and* at least five minutes a day praying *together* — as husband and wife at the same time — about any part of your marriage where you would like God's counsel and guidance. You may do this however you like. You may use formal or spontaneous prayer. If you would like to do more, please feel free to do so, but regardless, we are asking you to commit to a minimum of ten minutes a day of individual and couple prayer for your marriage.

2. Each and every day, think of some request or need that your spouse expresses, where your first instinct is to say no. Assuming that need or request is not immoral or personally demeaning in some way, take a deep breath and choose instead to say yes and *cheerfully* meet that need or request. If it's hard, ask for God's help in the moment. For example, use a simple prayer, called an aspiration, that goes like this: "Lord, help me love my spouse the way you love my spouse." Then make it happen. Here is one more condition. You may not keep score or brag about how well you did the exercise to each other. Each of you is responsible on your own before God to be faithful to this exercise because he is your First Spouse and he is asking *you* to learn to be the kind of spouse he would be to your mate. Keep your eyes on your own paper (so to speak).

Couples' Exercise:

- Heavenly Checkup

❧❧ HEAVENLY HULLABALOO

HEAVENLY CHECKUP

At the end of each week, evaluate your progress toward this Heavenly Habit. Discuss your answers with your spouse.

Week 1 _____

1. How effective were you at keeping your commitment to at least five minutes of individual prayer and five minutes of couple prayer each day?

   > Not at all effective 1 2 3 4 5 6 7 8 9 10 Totally effective

2. How effective were you at being more generous to requests to leave your comfort zone and love and serve your spouse in ways you have previously resisted?

   > Not at all effective 1 2 3 4 5 6 7 8 9 10 Totally effective

3. What, if anything, will you do this week to try to be more attentive to these habits or to build on the progress you have made so far?

Week 2 _____

1. How effective were you at keeping your commitment to at least five minutes of individual prayer and five minutes of couple prayer each day?

   > Not at all effective 1 2 3 4 5 6 7 8 9 10 Totally effective

2. How effective were you at being more generous to requests to leave your comfort zone and love and serve your spouse in ways you have previously resisted?

   > Not at all effective 1 2 3 4 5 6 7 8 9 10 Totally effective

3. What, if anything, will you do this week to try to be more attentive to these habits or to build on the progress you have made so far?

Week 3 _____

1. How effective were you at keeping your commitment to at least five minutes of individual prayer and five minutes of couple prayer each day?

> Not at all effective 1 2 3 4 5 6 7 8 9 10 Totally effective

2. How effective were you at being more generous to requests to leave your comfort zone and love and serve your spouse in ways you have previously resisted?

> Not at all effective 1 2 3 4 5 6 7 8 9 10 Totally effective

3. What, if anything, will you do this week to try to be more attentive to these habits or to build on the progress you have made so far?

Week 4 _____

1. How effective were you at keeping your commitment to at least five minutes of individual prayer and five minutes of couple prayer each day?

> Not at all effective 1 2 3 4 5 6 7 8 9 10 Totally effective

2. How effective were you at being more generous to requests to leave your comfort zone and love and serve your spouse in ways you have previously resisted?

> Not at all effective 1 2 3 4 5 6 7 8 9 10 Totally effective

3. What, if anything, will you do this week to try to be more attentive to these habits or to build on the progress you have made so far?

YOUR HEAVENLY MISSION FROM GOD

2

❧ OPENING THE SESSION

Summary of Session Two

Just as religious orders each have different charisms, ministries, and rules of life, each Heavenly Couple is called to develop its own identity in Christ. This session helps couples develop a marriage (and family) mission plan that connects the Christian virtues to specific new habits and actions the couple would like to develop to live their faith more fully in their particular circumstances. This exercise comprises the heart of the "little way" of marriage, allowing spirituality to be intimately connected to everything the couple does in the course of their day.

Opening Prayer

Leader: Let's begin in the name of the Father and of the Son and of the Holy Spirit.

All: Amen.

Leader: Lord Jesus Christ, we come before you today to give our hearts and minds and strength to you. In this second month of our commitment to learn your plan for marriage, help us to focus our eyes on you, the source and sustainer of our love for each other. Help us to remember that in everything we do, you ask us to keep our Christian virtues in mind so that in all decisions, big and small, we defer to you, our First Spouse.

Finally, Lord, we thank you for creating us with a divine purpose in mind. Help us to understand that purpose more fully and to help each other fulfill that purpose more completely in our marriage, so that our love may bear witness both to your glory and to your love for the world.

Let's take a moment to offer the prayers of our hearts to the Lord. We'll all pray together, "Lord, teach us your love."

Petition 1:	For all the couples here today, that we would understand and fulfill your purpose for our lives and our marriages. We pray to the Lord.
All:	Lord, teach us your love.
Petition 2:	Help us live out your plan for our marriages in all things, big and small, and help our relationships be an inspiration to those who struggle.
All:	Lord, teach us your love.
Petition 3:	Lord, help us remember to seek your guidance and the counsel of your Holy Spirit in all that we do in our marriages and family lives, so that you will be glorified in every aspect of our relationship.
All:	Lord, teach us your love.
Leader:	If anyone would like to offer a petition of your own, please speak up now. (*Pause for petitions.*)
Leader:	Lord, we give you every part of our life and marriage. We give you our communication, our decisions, our physical intimacy, our problems, our joys, and all the mundane aspects of our daily life. Give us the wisdom to discern your will in all of these areas, and give us the courage to follow your will wherever it leads us. We take a moment at this time to silently pray for the couple we selected at our first gathering. (*Moment of silence.*) We entrust our prayers to the intercession of your mother as we pray,
All:	Hail Mary . . . *Amen.*

Heavenly Witness

VIDEO AND DISCUSSION

Question #1:   What is a marital theme, and what is the one theme that will ensure the lifelong meaningfulness and intimacy of a couple's relationship?

Question #2: Practically speaking, how does a couple's marital theme affect their daily lives?

Question #3: What are the benefits to the marriage of keeping your marital imperative in mind as you make both big and small decisions about how you live out both your personal and your marital lives?

❦❦ GROUP DISCUSSION EXERCISE

Case Study

Leader: Kathy and Mark have been married for fourteen years and are the parents of three children, ages four, eight, and twelve. They rate the overall quality of their marriage as "good" but have reached an impasse over the last year that is causing a lot of tension.

Kathy is very happy with her daily life. She loves her neighbors, book club, and parish. She also feels that the children are getting an excellent education in their highly rated school district.

Mark, on the other hand, wants to move. While he enjoys his job as a manager at an office in the city, his passion is carpentry, specifically furniture building. Mark wants to buy several acres in the country where he can build a small carpentry shop and practice his hobby more effectively than in their suburban neighborhood.

"I'll keep my job in the city," Mark explains, "but I want a better quality of life during my off hours. I want to teach the kids how to build a tree house, maybe even to hunt a little. I'd like to own some farm animals. Maybe a horse or two, some chickens, maybe even a couple of goats. I think the kids would grow in responsibility and enjoy the freedom of country life. I think it would be a better, more wholesome lifestyle for the whole family. I work so hard all week. I think I deserve to be in a place I could enjoy on the weekends."

Kathy feels angrier and more frustrated every time Mark looks at the real estate page. "I can't believe he wants me to give up everything I have here.

He's not here all day. He doesn't understand what it takes to be the one raising three kids. We live in the best school district in the area. I think he would be severely compromising the children's education and futures by moving them to some country-bumpkin school system. On top of that, I would be the one sacrificing everything. My friends and activities are all here. Why should the children and I give up our whole lives for some dream that is going to take up all of Mark's evenings and weekends and leave me even more on my own?"

Discussion Questions

After learning about developing a marital imperative, Kathy and Mark decided that they wanted to be a couple who strives to live out the virtues of respectfulness, joy, faith, solidarity (family togetherness), and intimacy (emotional closeness).

Keeping these virtues in the forefront of your mind, how would you advise Kathy and Mark to solve their dilemma?

ACTIVITY

Heavenly Home Improvement Plan

1. Spend at least five minutes a day asking God to help you love your spouse the way he loves your mate, and spend at least five minutes a day praying together as a couple about any part of your marriage that you would like God's guidance about.

2. Each day say yes to some need or request from your spouse (assuming that it is not something that is demeaning or morally offensive) that you tend to naturally want to say no to.

3. In addition to continuing these habits, we would ask that you complete the Marital Imperative Exercise at the end of this unit in your workbook.

Couples' Exercise:

• **Marital Imperative Exercise**

HEAVENLY HULLABALOO

THE MARITAL IMPERATIVE EXERCISE

Directions: A marital imperative is a kind of marital mission statement centered around the virtues, moral ideals, and spiritual ideals you most want to be identified with throughout your life. Look at the list of virtues below. Most people want to be good examples of all of them, but it's difficult to grow in all of the virtues at the same time. Of the following virtues, which would best help you rise to the challenges you face in your daily marriage and family life? Choose two to four of the qualities listed (or identify others on your own in the space provided below) with which you would most like to be identified over the course of your life.

The Theological Virtues

These are virtues that enable us to know God and allow his life to be intertwined with ours.

_____ *Faith:* A free gift from God that allows you to be aware of his presence in your life and invites you to want him to become a greater part of your life.

_____ *Hope:* Confidence that God will never abandon or forsake you because neither death nor life, nor any living creature, nor any circumstance can come between you and his love.

_____ *Love:* The active choice to daily follow God's example and work for the good of another person whether or not you "feel" like it and even if it calls you to leave behind your comfort zone.

The Cardinal Virtues

Named for the Latin word for "hinge" (*cardine*), which refers to the four qualities on which a truly faithful and fruitful Christian life hinges.

_____ *Prudence* helps you discern the right time and the right way to act under any circumstance.

_____ *Justice* is a desire to make sure everybody in your family receives according to their level of need while at the same time contributes to the common good of your family to the fullest level of their ability. In parenting, it also means never using a more severe intervention when a lesser one will do the job sufficiently.

_____ *Temperance* gives you the ability to know how to enjoy your relationships and your possessions without allowing them to become a distraction or obsession.

_____ *Fortitude* is the ability to stay strong and do what you know is right even when others — or your own feelings — try to discourage you or dissuade you.

The Twelve Fruits of the Holy Spirit

These are virtues that should be present in those who are striving to live lives of faith.

__ Love	__ Patience	__ Faithfulness	__ Modesty
__ Joy	__ Kindness	__ Gentleness	__ Continence
__ Peace	__ Generosity	__ Self-Control	__ Chastity

Other Virtues of Value

___ Solidarity (a willingness to work together to help each other achieve a common and noble goal)

__ Hospitality	__ Openness	__ Knowledge	__ Creativity
__ Respect	__ Intimacy	__ Service	
__ Wisdom	__ Understanding	__ Supportiveness	

___ Fear of the Lord (joyful awe and respect at the power and goodness of God)

___ Piety (an acknowledgment of the respect we owe to God and sacred things)

List any other virtues you can think of here:

_____

_____

_____

Now combine the virtues you chose with the virtues chosen by your mate. Create your marital mission statement by completing the sentence below with the combined list of virtues.

As a couple we will strive to live out the virtues of _____

_____

_____ in our daily life.

Now, on your own, think of a few situations in which it would be helpful to have greater access to these virtues. (For example: when we argue about money, when I'm grumpy in the morning, when my spouse asks me to help with _____, etc.) Write them here.

_____

_____

_____

_____

If you could apply those virtues to the situations you identified above, how do think you would behave differently than you currently do?

_____

_____

_____

_____

Make a commitment to talk with your spouse each day about your successes and struggles in applying these virtues to the challenges you face throughout your day. What would be the best time of the day for these conversations? Write the time of day here. _____

Now speak the following promise aloud to each other and sign in the space below.

> [*Say your spouse's name.*]
> I genuinely respect the person that you are
> and the person God wants you to be.
> To that end, I promise that I will work
> to see the good in the things you value
> especially when I don't understand.
> I will never say that the dreams, goals, or values
> God has placed on your heart
> are silly, or unworthy of my time and attention.
> I promise to be the most important influence in your life
> second only to our Savior, Jesus Christ,
> because I love and honor who you are,
> and who God is calling you to become.
> I promise I will love and support you with all of my life
> all the days of my life.
> And I promise that with the Lord's help,
> I will be your best hope for arriving, properly attired,
> at the Heavenly Wedding Banquet.

_____   _____
            Husband   Wife

3

HEAVENLY COMMUNICATION

Plugging In to the Power of Grace

❧❧ OPENING THE SESSION

Summary of Session Three

Couples can't discern what God is calling them to become in their marriage and family if they aren't talking to him. This session addresses the importance of praying together, discusses ways to do this, and helps couples overcome resistances or obstacles to nurturing their prayer life.

Opening Prayer

Leader: Let's begin in the name of the Father and of the Son and of the Holy Spirit.

All: Amen.

Leader: Lord Jesus Christ, we come before you today to give our hearts and minds and strength to you. In this third month of our commitment to learn your plan for marriage, help us focus our eyes on you, the source and sustainer of our love for each other. Help us remember that in everything we do, you ask us to keep in mind your desire to be an active part of our marriage so that in all decisions, big and small, we consult you and defer to you, our First Spouse.

    Finally, Lord, help us overcome whatever discomfort we may feel as we learn to open our souls to you and to each other. Help us remember that it is only when we are comfortable sharing both our bodies and our souls with one another that the two become one. Give us the courage to take this leap of faith into each other's arms, and into a deeper life of grace. We ask this through Christ our Lord.

All: Amen.

Leader: Let's take a moment to offer the prayers of our hearts to the Lord. We'll all pray together, "Lord, draw us together in grace."

Petition 1:	For all the couples here today, that we would overcome the obstacles we place between you, our hearts, and our marriage. We pray to the Lord.
All:	Lord, draw us together in grace.
Petition 2:	Help us live out your plan for our marriages in all things, big and small, by learning to consult you, to hear your voice clearly, and to follow your will in our lives.
All:	Lord, draw us together in grace.
Petition 3:	Lord, help us remember that you are the source of our love and intimacy. Make us willing to place ourselves under your guidance so that we can fully celebrate every aspect of the love you give us.
All:	Lord, draw us together in grace.
Leader:	If anyone would like to offer a petition of your own, please speak up now. (*Pause for petitions.*)
Leader:	Lord, we give you every part of our life and marriage. We give you our communication, our decisions, our physical intimacy, our problems, our joys, and all the mundane aspects of our daily life. Give us the wisdom to discern your will in all of these areas, and give us the courage to follow your will wherever it leads us. We take a moment at this time to silently pray for the couple we selected at our first gathering. (*Moment of silence.*) We entrust our prayers to the intercession of your mother as we pray,
All:	Hail Mary … *Amen.*

Heavenly Witness

[*Say your spouse's name.*]
I genuinely respect the person that you are
and the person God wants you to be.
To that end, I promise that I will work
to see the good in the things you value
especially when I don't understand.
I will never say that the dreams, goals, or values
God has placed on your heart
are silly, or unworthy of my time and attention.
I promise to be the most important influence in your life
second only to our Savior, Jesus Christ,
because I love and honor who you are,
and who God is calling you to become.

I promise I will love and support you with all of my life
all the days of my life.
And I promise that with the Lord's help,
I will be your best hope for arriving, properly attired,
at the Heavenly Wedding Banquet.

3

❧❧ VIDEO AND DISCUSSION

Presentation of Focus Questions

Question #1:   What does plugging in to God's grace have to do with your capacity to love your mate?

Question #2:   How does couple prayer benefit a couple's ability to solve problems more effectively?

Question #3:   How can a couple decide what sort of spiritual practices will benefit them the most, and how do you evaluate whether a particular devotion or prayer form is "working" for a couple?

❧❧ GROUP DISCUSSION EXERCISE

Case Study

Jennifer and Gary have been married for five years. Jennifer is four months pregnant with their first child. "We've always had a pretty solid relationship," says Jennifer. "We have the typical struggles any couple has, you know — the occasional battle over bills, in-laws, chores. But mostly we get along great and have fun together.

"Over the last couple of months, I've started to want a little more. You know — go a little deeper. I think it's the baby. Knowing there's a new person growing inside me feels like such a miracle. I guess I'm thinking a lot more about God. Seeing my baby on our first sonogram just blew me away. When I left the doctor's office, I did something I've never done before. I went to the hospital chapel, knelt before the tabernacle, and just wept with gratitude. I feel close to God in a way I never have before. Oh, I've always gone to church on Sundays and believed in God, but I never felt a closeness like I did in that moment. I want more of that and I hope one day my child can have that kind of experience. I've been trying to take some time to pray when I have some time alone. I really want to share all this with Gary, but he seems kind of awkward when I try to talk about it, and he usually changes the subject."

"Jennifer is right about this baby changing us," Gary adds. "I've always been a pretty happy-go-lucky guy. I enjoy my friends, family. I'm even pretty happy with my job — well, most days, anyway. But suddenly, with the baby coming, I've started freaking out a little. I want so much for this child, and suddenly I feel so limited and small. I want so much to protect this new person from all the evils in the world. I've always gone to Mass on the 'big' days — ya know, Christmas, Easter. Since I've been married to Jennifer, I go every week. Her family has always gone every Sunday, so it's become something we always do — ten o'clock Mass followed by lunch with her parents. It's good. But since we found out we're pregnant, I've felt like I better kick it up a few notches. After all, I'm responsible for raising this person and keeping our child away from drugs, drinking, premarital sex, and so much other stuff. I feel like I really need God in my life for the first time. But I feel kind of stuck. We never discussed spiritual stuff in my family. Church was kind of more my mom's thing. My dad was a kind of self-made, stiff-upper-lip man. I never saw him pray, and I feel uncomfortable talking to Jennifer about all this. I want to, but I can't seem to get myself there."

Discussion Questions

1. Based on the information you gained from tonight's session — and any personal experience you may have had — what advice would you give Jennifer and Gary about starting to pray together in general?

2. Jennifer and Gary are really at a loss to identify the kinds of prayers they might say and the "best" way to pray. Identify some prayers, devotions, or prayer forms that have been meaningful to you or to people you know. Why do you think some people find these ways of praying meaningful? *Note*: If no one in your group has any experience with prayer or knows anyone with a meaningful prayer life, take a moment to write a prayer as a group that includes the following elements: (a) praise/gratitude for your marriage, (b) a request for help to live out married life fully, and (c) a commitment to do God's will. Write it in the space provided below. Commit to praying this every day with your spouse.

3. Neither Jennifer nor Gary feels very comfortable with couple prayer, even though they like the idea of it. What virtue or quality could they add to their marital imperative that might help them through this resistance? In what specific ways might this virtue or quality help them overcome their reluctance to pray together? (*Note*: For a list of some virtues, see the Marital Imperative Exercise on page 19 of your workbook.)

❦❦ ACTIVITY

Heavenly Home Improvement Plan

1. Each day say yes to some need or reasonable request from your spouse that you tend to naturally want to say no to.

2. Each day recall your marital imperative and the virtues you identified as being central to your married life. Ask yourself, "How can I apply these virtues to the challenges I will face today, and what additional virtues might I need to practice as well?"

3. And your new Heavenly Habit…

P	Praise and Thanksgiving
R	Repentance
A	Ask for your needs
I	Intercede for others
S	Seek God's will
E	Express your desire to serve him

In place of the previous assignment to spend five minutes a day in individual prayer and five minutes in couple prayer, daily use the PRAISE format both individually and with your mate. Add whatever formal prayers or devotions you would like. The first time you pray together, discuss any potential discomfort or resistance you may be experiencing as well as the virtues or qualities you will need to grow in as you learn to overcome this resistance. Continue to discuss your experience throughout the month, and make adjustments in your prayer time as necessary. *Once a week,* complete the Spiritual Checkup Exercise to help you stay in touch with each other about how your effort is affecting you and your relationship.

Tailor your prayer to meet your specific needs. Since it is intended to be a memory aid more than a required structure for prayer, you may even abandon the PRAISE format if you and your mate agree to do so, but make sure you keep all the elements of praise/thanksgiving, repentance, petition, and intercession, while seeking God's will and expressing a desire to serve him.

Couples' Exercise:

- **Heavenly Checkup**

 # HEAVENLY HULLABALOO

HEAVENLY CHECKUP EXERCISE

Directions: Each week respond to the following questions and discuss your answers with your mate.

Week 1 _____

1. How would you rate your comfort with praying together this week?

   > Extremely uncomfortable 1 2 3 4 5 6 7 8 9 10 Extremely comfortable

2. How would you rate your level of commitment to making couple prayer happen this week?

   > Very little effort 1 2 3 4 5 6 7 8 9 10 A great deal of effort

3. How would you rate the degree of your involvement in both actively praying and making improvements to your prayer time together?

   > Very little involvement 1 2 3 4 5 6 7 8 9 10 Very high involvement

4. What was the best experience you had with couple prayer this week? Why?

5. What changes would you make in your couple prayer time so that it could draw you even closer to each other and to God next week? Specifically, how do you think this change would be beneficial?

Week 2 _____

1. How would you rate your comfort with praying together this week?

   > Extremely uncomfortable 1 2 3 4 5 6 7 8 9 10 Extremely comfortable

2. How would you rate your level of commitment to making couple prayer happen this week?

> Very little effort 1 2 3 4 5 6 7 8 9 10 A great deal of effort

3. How would you rate the degree of your involvement in both actively praying and making improvements to your prayer time together?

> Very little involvement 1 2 3 4 5 6 7 8 9 10 Very high involvement

4. What was the best experience you had with couple prayer this week? Why?

5. What changes would you make in your couple prayer time so that it could draw you even closer to each other and to God next week? Specifically, how do you think this change would be beneficial?

Week 3

1. How would you rate your comfort with praying together this week?

> Extremely uncomfortable 1 2 3 4 5 6 7 8 9 10 Extremely comfortable

2. How would you rate your level of commitment to making couple prayer happen this week?

> Very little effort 1 2 3 4 5 6 7 8 9 10 A great deal of effort

3. How would you rate the degree of your involvement in both actively praying and making improvements to your prayer time together?

> Very little involvement 1 2 3 4 5 6 7 8 9 10 Very high involvement

4. What was the best experience you had with couple prayer this week? Why?

5. What changes would you make in your couple prayer time so that it could draw you even closer to each other and to God next week? Specifically, how do you think this change would be beneficial?

Week 4 _____

1. How would you rate your comfort with praying together this week?

Extremely uncomfortable 1 2 3 4 5 6 7 8 9 10 Extremely comfortable

2. How would you rate your level of commitment to making couple prayer happen this week?

Very little effort 1 2 3 4 5 6 7 8 9 10 A great deal of effort

3. How would you rate the degree of your involvement in both actively praying and making improvements to your prayer time together?

Very little involvement 1 2 3 4 5 6 7 8 9 10 Very high involvement

4. What was the best experience you had with couple prayer this week? Why?

5. What changes would you make in your couple prayer time so that it could draw you even closer to each other and to God next week? Specifically, how do you think this change would be beneficial?

4

HEAVENLY RAPPORT

Winning the Battle of the Sexes

OPENING THE SESSION

Summary of Session Four

Some husbands and wives feel as if they are speaking different languages. Heavenly Couples know what it means to be "flesh of my flesh and bone of my bone." This session draws from the theology of the body to explore the real vs. the false differences between man and woman. Briefly, real differences are those differences created by God that help men and women work better together because of those differences. False differences are those that arrived after the Fall and cause men and women to feel estranged from one another. Couples learn how the graces of marriage empower them to speak a new, shared language whose vocabulary is love and whose grammar is service. Through this, the couple strives toward the complementarity and original unity enjoyed by our first parents, Adam and Eve.

Opening Prayer

Leader: Let's begin in the name of the Father and of the Son and of the Holy Spirit.

All: Amen.

Leader: Lord Jesus Christ, we come before you today to give our hearts and minds and strength to you. In this fourth month of our commitment to learn your plan for marriage, help us learn the truth behind why you created us male and female. You gave Adam and Eve to one another to be perfect helpmates and companions, flesh of each other's flesh and bone of each other's bone. But sin entered into the world and destroyed that original unity between man and woman. Still, you gave us the sacrament of marriage to overcome the barriers of sin and to enable husbands and wives to climb out of the wreckage of selfishness and learn to once again be at peace and unity with one another. Help us seek that peace and unity. Teach us to leave behind the language of selfishness and separation. In its place, teach us to speak your words of generosity, service, and love to one another so that we might glorify you by becoming the helpmates you call every married couple to be. We ask this through Christ our Lord.

All: Amen.

Leader: Let's take a moment to offer the prayers of our hearts to the Lord. We'll all pray together, "Lord, make us one in you."

Petition 1:   For all the couples here today, that we would overcome the false differences which separate men and women and instead celebrate our true and complementary differences that enable us to image you and work together more perfectly. We pray to the Lord.

All: Lord, make us one in you.

Petition 2:   Give us the desire to seek an uncommon unity, so that we can celebrate an awesome love for one another and bear witness to the world of the unifying power of your grace.

All: Lord, make us one in you.

Petition 3:   Teach us to speak your words to one another and send your Holy Spirit to bridge the gaps that exist between our hearts.

All: Lord, make us one in you.

Leader: If anyone would like to offer a petition of your own, please speak up now. (*Pause for petitions.*)

Leader: Lord, you gave man and woman to each other to be perfect helpmates. Help us tonight as we discover what is necessary to celebrate a godly unity with one another. Give us the courage we need to leave behind the comfortable but false differences which separate us, while embracing those differences which draw us together in you. We take a moment at this time to silently pray for the couple we selected at our first gathering. (*Moment of silence.*) We entrust our prayers to the intercession of your mother as we pray,

All: Hail Mary ... *Amen.*

Heavenly Witness

VIDEO AND DISCUSSION

Question #1: How is it that men and women have come to feel they are so different from one another, and what was God's plan for them from the beginning?

Question #2: How can we distinguish the true differences between men and women, which were created by God, from the false differences, which are merely the result of sin?

Question #3: What is the "new language" that men and women must learn if they are to be the helpmates and intimate partners God intends them to be? How, and from whom, do they learn to speak this language?

GROUP DISCUSSION EXERCISE

Case Study

Lin and Phil have been married for six years. They have a four-year-old son and a two-year-old daughter. They came to Dr. Popcak's office seeking guidance for a situation they felt was deteriorating the quality of their marriage.

"I think we have a pretty good marriage overall," Lin began. "Phil is fun to be with. He's a good provider and a good dad. But lately we've been getting into these battles that never seem to go anywhere. It seems to have really taken off after our second child was born. I quit my job to be home full-time with the kids. It was very different for me. Suddenly I was counting on Phil for so much more. Not just income, but friendship as well. I didn't have a bunch of adults to share my day with anymore. Now I need Phil to bring some of the adult world home to me. Don't get me wrong, I love being home with the kids. But I can't wait to hear full English sentences by the end of the day! I also need to share the joys and frustrations of my day with him. Lately, I haven't really felt like Phil wants to hear about it, or share with me very much. It makes me feel lonely and vulnerable. I've tried talking to him about it, but he just doesn't seem to get it.

"In addition, I've really noticed that Phil just doesn't 'get' how to parent a daughter. It was hard for me at first when our son became a toddler. Phil would wrestle and roughhouse with him a lot. If our son got bumped or fell, Phil would tell him to 'Just rub it away, big guy.' I always wanted to run in and kiss the boo-boo, but I figured Phil knew more about being a boy than I did, so I held back. Now with our daughter, I can't do that. It really irritates me when he won't cuddle her when she cries. I want him to have tea parties with her and read her stories, not wrestle. I really get upset when I try to discuss it and he just blows me off and tells me that stuff is my job.

"When Phil and I were first dating, I was really attracted to his analytical mind and steady personality. Now I think all that steadiness is just a mask for his inability to share his feelings. I don't want this to wreck our family, but it's all building up, and I get more and more upset every time I see new evidence of it."

Phil jumped into the conversation at this point. "It's the 'more and more upset' that's getting to me," he shared. "When Lin was working, this wasn't as big a deal. We would talk about what happened that day. Laugh about the crazy people at work. No big deal. If she was having trouble on a project, I really enjoyed helping her find a solution. I got a lot of satisfaction from that. Now things seem different. When she says she feels vulnerable, that rings true. We can't seem to discuss much without her getting upset. She'll come to me with a problem she's had with the kids' behavior that day. I'll try to help her find a solution, and she'll get mad at me and tell me I don't understand how she feels. I think I do. She's frustrated—let's find a solution and fix the problem. But she ends up crying and telling me that I don't understand how hard it is to be a mom. I think all the hysterics are just making the job harder.

"As for the tea party thing, I just don't get that at all. I am who I am. I don't have one personality for boys and another for girls. Why do I have to change and do things like tea parties? It's not like Lin learned to play football just because she had a son. I just want to get to a place where everything doesn't end in her crying. I can see that as time has gone on, I've pulled away more and more. But I do it to balance all of her emotionality. One of us has to stay sane and steady. If I get upset every time there's a problem like she does, it would be chaos in our house. I don't want to lose Lin, but I feel like I need to keep her at arm's length sometimes to protect myself from getting sucked in when she's feeling upset."

Lin added, "He doesn't understand me, and I just don't get where he's coming from. What I'm asking doesn't seem so hard to me. I just don't know if there's any hope for this to get any better. I know men and women are different from each other. Maybe this is just as good as it gets."

Discussion Questions

1. Applying what you've just learned about the real vs. false differences between men and women, what are the unique strengths and perspectives (i.e., "real differences") that Phil and Lin can offer to help each other find greater balance? If each were more open to each other's strengths and perspectives as man and woman, how would they be able to approach the problem described more efficiently and effectively?

2. What, in your opinion, are the false differences/stereotypes (either traditional — i.e., "Man only breadwinner / Woman only child care giver" or modern — i.e., "Men and women are exactly the same") that Lin and Phil are clinging to? How are those stereotypes stopping them from being open to incorporating the unique gifts and strengths that each brings to the table as man and woman?

3. What are the concrete actions Lin and Phil could take if they were to more effectively apply their unique masculine and feminine strengths to the problem at hand?

☙☙ ACTIVITY

Heavenly Home Improvement Plan

1. Each day say yes to some need or reasonable request from your spouse that you tend to naturally want to say no to.

2. Each day recall your marital imperative and the virtues you identified as being central to your married life. Ask yourself, "How can I apply these virtues to the challenges I will face today, and what additional virtues might I need to practice as well?"

3. Keep up your daily individual and couple prayer time. Keep using the PRAISE format unless you have mutually decided to do something else. Continue to discuss your experience throughout the month, and make adjustments in your prayer time as necessary.

4. And your new Heavenly Habit...

Refer to the Heavenly Rapport Exercise on the next page. In that exercise, you will ask yourself, "What are the emotional, spiritual, relational, or practical tasks of living out my life and relationship that I have previously refused to do — or never thought of trying to do — because that wasn't what other men and women do for their mates?" Discuss with your spouse whether he or she would appreciate your developing greater competency in those areas. Assuming that your mate would appreciate this, think about how you would learn to be more competent in this area. Also, reflect on the virtues you will need to practice in developing this competency. Add these virtues to your marital imperative.

At the end of this session, there are thirty optional discussion questions and action suggestions designed to help you get the most out of the focus of tonight's Heavenly Date Night: Heavenly Rapport. Do as many of them as you like to maximize the potential for Heavenly Rapport in your marriage.

Couples' Exercises:

- **Heavenly Rapport Exercise**
- **Help! I Feel Like I'm Losing Myself**

☙☙ HEAVENLY HULLABALOO

HEAVENLY RAPPORT EXERCISE

This month you are invited to learn the new language based on mutual love and service that God intended men and women to speak to one another from the very beginning. As with learning any new language, sometimes it may be challenging, and you'll have to be patient with one another. But as you become more comfortable with the vocabulary of love and the grammar of service, the rewards will be a deep intimacy and trust between you and your mate, as well as a stronger personal sense of what it means to be a mature man or woman of God.

1. Ask yourself, "What are the emotional, spiritual, relational, or practical tasks of living out my life and relationship that I have previously refused to do — or never thought of trying to do — because, in your estimation, that wasn't what other men and women do for their mates?" In particular, consider the following areas of your relationship:

Spirituality and Prayer:

Emotional Communication (e.g., sharing hopes and dreams, offering feedback about thoughts and feelings, discussing struggles of your day, discussing your problems and struggles, etc.):

Sexuality and Physical Intimacy (excluding those things which are contrary to Catholic teaching. If you don't know what that entails, please refer to the *Catechism of the Catholic Church* or books like *Holy Sex* by Dr. Gregory Popcak or *Good News About Sex and Marriage* by Christopher West):

Parenting:

Domestic Chores and Household Responsibilities:

Finances/Budgeting:

Other Areas of Personal Importance:

2. Discuss with your spouse whether he or she would appreciate your developing greater competency in those areas. What specifically would he or she like you to do to be more helpful?

3. If your mate agrees that becoming more competent in these areas would be beneficial to him or her, identify the *specific* action steps you'd like to take to learn how to be more competent in these areas.

4. Ask yourself if you think you might require additional support or training in order to develop these skills or abilities (e.g., spiritual direction, counseling, other specific instruction/classes). What steps will you take to locate these resources in your area?

5. What are the qualities or virtues you will be practicing as you develop the skills you listed in point #1 above? Describe how you feel living out those virtues through the body God gave you to make you a more mature and authentic man or woman of God. Add those virtues to your marital imperative.

6. In addition to the exercise above, each morning, before your start your day, ask each other the following question: "What can I do to make your day easier or more pleasant?"

HELP! I FEEL LIKE I'M LOSING MYSELF

Sometimes as couples work to learn this new language of mutual love and generous service, they feel like they are either "not being true to themselves" or "losing themselves." This feeling simply means that previously, this person has tended not to find their identity in the virtues of which God created them to be a living, breathing example, but rather their own petty comforts and preferences. This sense of "losing oneself" is what it feels like to do what Jesus commands all of his followers to do when he says that we must learn to "die to ourselves." But when we embrace this process, instead of losing ourselves, we discover who we really are! We discover that we are not mere animals, bound by our own comforts and petty preferences. We are sons and daughters of the Most High God, called to bear witness to the eternal virtues which contain the secrets of a happy life, an intimate marriage, and eternal life itself.

If you are struggling to live out the principles contained within this exercise, or any of the exercises that challenge you to leave behind your comfort zone for the sake of becoming who you really are, *be encouraged*. It's a challenge worth facing. Don't believe what the world tells you. You are more than the sum of your likes and dislikes. Do not find your identity in what you like or what makes you comfortable today — for all these things will pass away or fail you at some point. Instead, find your identity in Christ, by living out the eternal virtues that make you a son or daughter of God.

Below are a list of optional activities you may choose to do throughout the month to come to a better understanding of how to more effectively apply the real differences between men and women (as opposed to the false ones) to the challenges of everyday life.

Day 1: Just challenging preconceived notions of men's and women's roles is only the first step. The most important thing is moving outside of preconceived ideas onto things that will make your particular marriage more intimate and rewarding. Therefore, each of you should create a list of things that you would like help with in your daily life. This is not to be a complaint list. No "*You never*'s" or "*Why don't you*'s." Simply make a wish list.

Day 2: Exchange your lists. No reactions allowed. Just take them and read them alone. You don't have to do them all. However, the lists will be great reminders of the needs on a day-to-day basis. Try to add the tasks that you are physically capable of to your activities. Even one new activity a week is a good start.

Day 3: Discuss with your spouse the different roles your parents played in their marriages. How have their examples impacted your ideas of men's and women's roles?

Day 4: Today, instead of concentrating on the work you would like help with, make a list of the things you think are the most *fun* to do. Some of the things, you might already do with your spouse, others may be things your spouse hasn't shown an interest in before. List as many fun things as you can think of, including things you think would be fun but have never tried before. (Again, no complaints. Just concentrate on what would be fun.)

Day 5: Exchange your lists. Again, read them alone. Pick one that you've never done with your spouse before, especially if you haven't tried it because you think "guys don't do that" or "girls don't do that." Schedule a date to do that thing with your spouse as soon as possible. (You will now have two dates on your schedules, one for each of you to try something new. Remember you are loving your spouse in a generous way. Do this with your best attitude. No complaining or grouching.)

Day 6: Discuss the chores you were assigned as a child. Were they the same as or different from those of your siblings of the opposite sex? How did this affect the chores you naturally do today?

Day 7: Create a list of emotional needs you have met by others outside your marriage. For example: wife might list things like, "My girlfriends understand my frustrations as a mother." Husband might list things like, "The guys help me to blow off steam. I can just have fun without thinking too hard."

Day 8: Exchange lists. Read them alone. Resist the temptation to feel threatened by the other relationships in your spouse's life. We all need a community. We will discuss this later in the session on faithfulness. For now think of ways you might do some of the things that other people do for your spouse emotionally. For example: do you need to listen more to the stories of your spouse's daily life? (Hint: just because it's not what you do all day, or what you've been educated in, doesn't mean it's boring.) Do you need to lighten up a bit and have more fun? Challenge yourself to do some of these things for your spouse, especially the ones that make you role your eyes and groan.

Day 9: Discuss some of the real differences between you and your spouse. They can be physical (one of you may be taller or stronger or more energetic than the other) or more emotional in nature (one of you may have a great sense of humor, or one of you may be more naturally empathetic). Make a point of thanking your spouse for sharing these gifts with you.

Day 10: Hopefully, you have been trying to do some of the things on the lists you exchanged on day 2. If not, pick another chore from the list and do it cheerfully.

Day 11: Write your spouse a thank-you note for working with you on this session. List a few of the things they've done that you know have been more challenging for them, or that you've been impressed by.

Day 12: When people get married, we often think that the doing of certain work just comes with the package. This attitude kills the gratitude we should have for all that our spouses do for us. Meditate for a few minutes on all the extra things you would be doing if you were suddenly single, yet all the responsibilities of your present life remained. Make it a habit to thank your spouse for the contributions he/she makes. It may feel silly at first to say, "Honey, thanks for going to work today" or, "Thanks for doing the laundry" or, "Thanks for changing that diaper." However, everything your spouse does in a day is a gift of self. Express your appreciation.

Day 13: Time to get out your calendars again. Pick one item off of each of your fun lists and schedule dates to do them.

Day 14: Who is one person of your gender whose qualities you really admire? The person can be someone you know, a famous person, or a character in a book or movie. List those qualities and why you find them attractive. How can you incorporate some of those qualities into your life? How would doing so benefit your marriage?

Day 15: Emotional checkup day. Are you trying to meet the emotional needs your spouse listed on day 7? Recommit to the effort to do them.

Day 16: Financial stress in marriage often comes from what we learned from our parents about money. Check out some of the books by Suze Orman on dealing with the emotional side of money. Discuss how each of your childhood experiences has shaped how you deal with finances in adulthood. Don't argue over what to do next; just share the information. Later on, check out Phil Lenahan's work on money management for Catholics.

Day 17: Discuss what each of you thinks are the differences in how men and women parent. When each of you brings your unique gifts and talents to parenting, how do you complement each other?

Day 18: Write your spouse a love note. Let them know which of their qualities you really find attractive. List as many as you can.

Day 19: Sometimes a spouse truly doesn't have the time or ability to help with a chore that may be on your list. Discuss how together you can solve this problem. Be creative and work together.

Day 20: Schedule two more fun dates from your list.

Day 21: Discuss how your parents parented you. How did their styles reflect the true and false differences between men and women? How has this affected your parenting style? Are there things you would like to change about your parenting style in light of the information in this session? If so, what?

Day 22: Society of Ten classifies movies, TV shows, and books into men's and women's categories. Pick a movie, show, or book that one of you has enjoyed but the other wanted no part of because it was a guy or girl thing. Watch or read it together. Find at least two things you appreciated about the other's choice. (Nothing morally objectionable, please.)

Day 23: Are there preconceived ideas about boys and girls that have influenced how you have parented your children? In light of the session, is their anything you think you should change? If your children are grown, is there anything you would go back and change if you could? If you don't have children yet, is there something you would like to keep in mind if you are ever blessed with children? Discuss.

Day 24: Have you been challenging yourself to do some of the jobs on your spouse's help list? If not, pick a new one and do it cheerfully.

Day 25: Are there any fun things that one of you enjoys doing with your kids that the other opts out of because it's just not feminine or masculine? With a positive attitude, give it a try. To the other spouse: participate, too, and be loving and supportive of the other's efforts.

Day 26: Write your spouse a love note describing which of their physical traits you find to be most masculine (husband) or feminine (wife). How do these traits attract you? Be appreciative and romantic.

Day 27: Emotional checkup day.

Day 28: Remember to thank your spouse for doing some of those things you are not physically gifted at doing.

Day 29: Schedule two more fun dates, one from each of your lists.

Day 30: Discuss how, if at all, your views of men's and women's roles have changed over the month. Are there more or fewer real differences than you originally thought? What are the differences/similarities you've come to appreciate most about your spouse?

5

HEAVENLY LOVE

Supercharging Friendship and Intimacy

❧❧ OPENING THE SESSION

Summary of Session Five

Some couples think that love is a feeling and that if they don't feel loving, then acting loving is "dishonest." Heavenly Couples know that love is the commitment to work for the good of one's spouse even at the risk of one's own comfort. This session explores obstacles to real love and provides action steps that the couple can use to increase their experience of real love in their relationship.

Opening Prayer

Leader:	Let's begin in the name of the Father and of the Son and of the Holy Spirit.
All:	Amen.
Leader:	Lord Jesus Christ, we come before you today to give our hearts and minds and strength to you. In this fifth month of our commitment to learn your plan for marriage, help us to learn how to live the close, intimate friendship you intended for all husbands and wives. Help us to work for each other's good in all that we do, even when doing so requires us to step outside of what makes us comfortable. Help us to be both passionate friends *and* lovers to one another, so that we can be the physical reminders of the passion and friendship you extend to each of us. Finally, help us to remember that of all the things we do each day, loving each other is the most important task. We ask this through Christ our Lord.
All:	Amen.
Leader:	Let's take a moment to offer the prayers of our hearts to the Lord. We'll all pray together, "Lord, teach us your friendship and love."

Petition 1:	Lord, in your generosity, you raise us up and call us your friends. Help us to live the fullness of Christian friendship in our married lives.
All:	Lord, teach us your friendship and love.
Petition 2:	Teach us to understand the divine purpose of both companionate and romantic love, and enable us to live both fully each and every day.
All:	Lord, teach us your friendship and love.
Petition 3:	Lord, so many things compete for our attention. Help us always to remember to prioritize our marriage and family life, so that we never take each other for granted or make each other question the love we share.
All:	Lord, teach us your friendship and love.
Leader:	If anyone would like to offer a petition of your own, please speak up now. (*Pause for petitions.*)
Leader:	Lord, in your goodness, you have called us your friends. Strengthen us through the grace of marriage to be true friends to one another. Enable each husband and wife to be intimate friends and passionate lovers to each other. Fill our homes with playfulness, joy, attentiveness, care, thoughtfulness, and a heartfelt concern for one another. And enable us to celebrate the kind of love that can carry us through difficulties and make each day together a gift. We take a moment at this time to silently pray for the couple we selected at our first gathering. (*Moment of silence.*) We entrust our prayers to the intercession of your mother as we pray,
All:	Hail Mary . . . *Amen.*

Heavenly Witness

🐦🐦 VIDEO AND DISCUSSION

Question #1: What is "companionate love," and what is its role in marriage?

Question #2:   What is "romantic love," and what is its role in marriage?

Question #3:   What are the three lovestyles, and how can mastering each other's lovestyles help you to both love each other better and grow as persons?

❧❧ GROUP DISCUSSION EXERCISE

Case Study

Judy and Chuck met at the opening of a mutual friend's art gallery. Chuck is an architect. Judy teaches art at the university level. They hit it off fairly quickly, and were married eight months later.

"We have so much in common," says Judy. "We enjoy a lot of the same things. We spend our weekends going to art shows, or trolling around antique shops looking for just the right pieces for our apartment. We have very similar tastes, and it's a lot of fun to work on projects together, like spending the evenings talking about our days while we refinish some great old piece of furniture together. We really enjoy each other's company."

"She's great," Chuck chimes in. "It's so wonderful to have someone who *gets* me. I appreciate her input on my work. I feel like I'm doing the best work of my life since we've been together. I love the life we're building together."

"Things are great most of the time," says Judy. "But when we hit a rough patch, like when my mom was hospitalized for pneumonia last month, or when Chuck hit a major snag with one of his top clients awhile back, we seem to drift apart. I want us to be there for the hard times, as well as the fun. I feel like those are the times when we really need to talk things out, share ideas, discuss plans for how we're going to get through whatever we're going through together, but Chuck seems to go off into his own head when he gets stressed. That's hard for me. I really needed him to be there for me, to talk through my concerns and listen to my frustrations."

"I don't mean to neglect Judy when I get stressed. I just need some peace and quiet so I can puzzle everything out," Chuck responds. "When we're going through a rough patch, I just want to go work out by myself or do something to work off the negative energy I'm feeling. I just don't feel like talking then."

These differences seem to affect other areas of their relationship as well. Judy says, "Sometimes I don't feel as emotionally connected as I'd like. Sometimes I'll just want to give him a call at the office and say, 'I love you.' Or I'll just want to stay up and talk about stuff, but he says he's too tired. It's okay because I know he loves me. He leaves little notes sometimes, or brings me flowers, and he's always looking for ways he can help out or do things. I just don't feel like I know his heart."

Chuck responds, "I get what she's saying, and that's fair, I guess. For my end, she isn't as affectionate as I'd like her to be. Sexually, things are great, but I just wish she'd be more comfortable holding my hand in public or hanging out with me and just being close on the couch together. But she's always popping up to do something or straighten something. Things are good, but I think they could be better. I just don't think either of us is really sure what to do."

Discussion Questions

1. While some of the differences between Chuck and Judy could be explained in part by common differences between men and women, focus for a moment on the lovestyles that are coming into play. Which of the three lovestyles (visual, auditory, kinesthetic) do Chuck and Judy have in common? What are the lovestyles that Chuck and Judy do not share as much?

2. Although becoming more proficient in a different lovestyle can be challenging, with a willing heart and some effort, it is possible to harmonize differing lovestyles more effectively. What things could Judy do to practice being more proficient with the kinesthetic lovestyle? What could Chuck do to become more proficient in the auditory lovestyle? How could each person find out what actions would be most meaningful to the other? What are gentle ways that you could suggest Chuck and Judy use to remind each other when they forget to reach out to each other through all the different lovestyles?

☙☙ ACTIVITY

5

Heavenly Home Improvement Plan

1. Each day say yes to some need or reasonable request from your spouse that you tend to naturally want to say no to.

2. Each day recall your marital imperative and the virtues you identified as being central to your married life. Ask yourself, "How can I apply these virtues to the challenges I will face today, and what additional virtues might I need to practice as well?"

3. Keep up your daily individual and couple prayer time. Keep using the PRAISE format unless you have mutually decided to do something else. Continue to discuss your experience throughout the month, and make adjustments in your prayer time as necessary.

4. Keep looking for new ways to work together so that you can apply all the gifts of being a man or a woman to the problems, tasks, and challenges you face every day.

5. And your new Heavenly Habit…

Become an expert in your mate's lovestyle. Take a moment to look on the following page and review the Lovestyle Quiz. Complete the quiz and follow the directions to learn more about how understanding each other's lovestyles can improve your marriage.

Do the Heavenly Checkup following the Lovestyle Quiz to evaluate your attentiveness to your mate's lovestyle.

Couples' Exercise:

- Lovestyle Quiz
- Heavenly Checkup

☙☙ HEAVENLY HULLABALOO

LOVESTYLE QUIZ

Directions: Check the statements that describe how you feel most of the time.

Visual Lovestyle:

___ Flowers, love notes, cards, etc. are most meaningful (not merely liked).

___ "Presentation" is important. (i.e., presents wrapped beautifully, meals presented on a well-set table).

___ Clothes that look good are more important than practicality or comfort.

___ You have a flair for decorating, fashion, or other visual arts.

___ Your "turn-ons" include things like candlelight, romantic surroundings, and wearing attractive pajamas or lingerie.

___ Personal appearance is very important.

___ You clean or tidy up when stressed.

___ You tend to be detail-oriented.

___ A house that looks clean is more important to you than a house that is clean.

___ You are very productive and can mentally track a million projects at once.

Auditory Lovestyle:

___ You talk constantly about everything.

___ You like hearing "I love you" or similar comments a million times a day.

___ The more you talk with someone, the closer you feel to them.

___ You're very sensitive to other's tone of voice or word choice.

___ Under stress, it's important to you to talk things out.

___ "If you take time to talk with me, that means you love me."

___ You are "turned on" by romantic/emotional/sexual conversations and/or "sweet nothings."

___ You often "just stopped to talk for a minute."

___ You need background noise (radio, TV always on even when you aren't paying attention to it).

___ Sounds/music/tone of voice affect your mood.

Kinesthetic Lovestyle

___ Physical affection is the most important way to feel connected.

___ You love just being quiet and "being" together.

___ You dress primarily for comfort. Appearance is secondary if considered at all.

___ You tend to feel overwhelmed and shut down in arguments or long conversations.

___ You tend not to reason things out, and give "gut" reactions to things.

___ You like to work off the stress physically, either through exercise or hard work.

___ "Why do we have to work so hard on the relationship? Can't we just let it be?"

___ You are "turned on" by touching, hugging, kissing, massage, and other physical contact.

___ You may have a hard time not going "all the way" when affection starts.

___ You may hate making plans. ("Can't we just wait and see what we *feel* like doing that day?"

___ You tend to be a poor organizer and/or don't notice messes or disorder.

Scoring: Count the number of checks in each category.

In which category did you mark the most checks?

_____ Visual   _____ Auditory   _____ Kinesthetic

This represents your primary lovestyle.

In which category did you mark the second most checks?

_____ Visual   _____ Auditory   _____ Kinesthetic

This represents your secondary lovestyle.

In which category do you have the least number of checks?

_____ Visual   _____ Auditory   _____ Kinesthetic

If you and your spouse differ in your primary and secondary lovestyles, please list ideas for things you can do to increase your proficiency in the lovestyles that are mismatched. For examples and additional ideas, please see chapter 7 of *For Better . . . FOREVER!**

*This quiz has been adapted from the Lovestyles chapter in *For Better . . . FOREVER! A Catholic Guide to Lifelong Marriage.*

HEAVENLY CHECKUP

At the end of each week, evaluate your progress toward this Heavenly Habit. Discuss your answers with your spouse.

Week 1 _____

1. How effectively do you feel you have attended to your mate's primary lovestyle this week?

Not at all effective 1 2 3 4 5 6 7 8 9 10 Totally effective

2. What, if anything, will you do this week to try to be more attentive to these habits or to build on the progress you have made so far?

Week 2 _____

1. How effectively do you feel you have attended to your mate's primary lovestyle this week?

Not at all effective 1 2 3 4 5 6 7 8 9 10 Totally effective

2. What, if anything, will you do this week to try to be more attentive to these habits or to build on the progress you have made so far?

Week 3 _____

1. How effectively do you feel you have attended to your mate's primary lovestyle this week?

> Not at all effective 1 2 3 4 5 6 7 8 9 10 Totally effective

2. What, if anything, will you do this week to try to be more attentive to these habits or to build on the progress you have made so far?

Week 4 _____

1. How effectively do you feel you have attended to your mate's primary lovestyle this week?

> Not at all effective 1 2 3 4 5 6 7 8 9 10 Totally effective

2. What, if anything, will you do this week to try to be more attentive to these habits or to build on the progress you have made so far?

6

HEAVENLY PROBLEM SOLVING

Getting Out of Your Own Way

❦❦ OPENING THE SESSION

Summary of Session Six

Just as the cross became the means of salvation, conflict in marriage — if engaged in correctly — can be the means by which a couple is led to the fullness of love. While some couples experience arguments as boxing matches or wars of attrition, Heavenly Couples experience conflict as a deep muscle massage that can be uncomfortable at the time, but leaves the relationship freer and more flexible afterward. In this session, the principles of Heavenly Problem Solving are explored, and couples develop action steps that will enable them to celebrate strengths and shore up weaknesses.

Opening Prayer

Leader: Let's begin in the name of the Father and of the Son and of the Holy Spirit.

All: Amen.

Leader: Lord Jesus Christ, sometimes love means celebrating joys and sharing our happiness. Often it means picking up our crosses and following after you. When we are having disagreements, arguments, and struggles, help us to lay aside what each of us wants, and take time to listen to your will for our lives together. When our homes and hearts are filled with discord, help us to achieve the peace beyond all understanding. Help us to remember that conflict does not mean that our marriage is failing, but that you are grinding away our imperfections in your refining fire. Take our iron and make us silver. Take our brass, and make us gold. And when the fires become too hot, send us your angel to guide us, and like Shadrach, Meshach, and Abednego of old, draw us safely out of the flames so that we might be a witness to the glory of your love in our lives.

                 We ask this through Christ our Lord.

All:	Amen.
Leader:	Let's take a moment to offer the prayers of our hearts to the Lord. We'll all pray together, "Lord, let us love through good times and bad."
Petition 1:	Lord, we are often frightened by each other's anger and hurt by each other's imperfections. Give us the peace beyond all understanding so that where there is anger, we may experience your love.
All:	Lord, let us love through good times and bad.
Petition 2:	Teach us to understand the divine purpose of conflict, and through our struggles, help us to achieve the unity you desire for us.
All:	Lord, let us love through good times and bad.
Petition 3:	Lord, help us to overcome our pettiness. Give us thick skins to prevent us from reacting needlessly to slights, and give us a light step to prevent us from treading on each others' feet. Finally Lord, give us the wisdom to know when to speak up and when to offer it up.
All:	Lord, let us love through good times and bad.
Leader:	If anyone would like to offer a petition of your own, please speak up now. (*Pause for petitions.*)
Leader:	Lord, each of us gathered here tonight is your bride, and you long for the day when we will celebrate our eternal wedding feast with you. Until then, help us to take advantage of every opportunity to use the conflict we encounter to rub away every blemish, bump, and imperfection of our character and spirits, so that when we arrive to meet you at our wedding banquet, we can stand confidently under your gaze, knowing that because of our spouse's intervention, we will be pleasing to your sight. We take a moment at this time to silently pray for the couple we selected at our first gathering. (*Moment of silence.*) We entrust our prayers to the intercession of your mother as we pray,
All:	Hail Mary … *Amen.*

Heavenly Witness

᪥᪥ VIDEO AND DISCUSSION

6

Presentation of Focus Questions

Question #1:   What is the spiritual purpose of conflict?

Question #2:   What is the one thing that every couple tries to do but only makes things worse? What is the healthy alternative?

Question #3:   What are the techniques presented that can help you and your mate solve problems gracefully?

Here are the tips presented in the video.

1. Watch your temperature before you start a discussion with your mate.

2. Watch your temperature during discussions with your mate.

3. Take breaks early, while you are still focused on solutions.

4. Remember your spouse is not the problem; the problem is the problem.

5. Always look for the positive intention behind the offensive behavior, not as a way of excusing the behavior, but as a charitable way to begin a discussion about changing that behavior.

6. Never negotiate the "what." Always negotiate the "how" and the "when."

7. If you need a deeper explanation of the tips in the video or would like more ideas about how to solve problems respectfully, check out the chapter in *For Better...FOREVER!* titled, "Red Hot Loving: How to Be Loving When Conflict Heats Things Up."

8. If a couple has difficulty applying the tips in the presentation or the ones they pick up in their independent reading, and their arguments consistently bring more pain than peace, they should seek competent, faithful help immediately.

❧❧ GROUP DISCUSSION EXERCISE

Case Study

1. Mitch and Barbara both have hot tempers. They tend to take things personally, and react strongly to perceived slights. The other day, Mitch forgot to replace the toilet paper roll, which precipitated a twenty-minute lecture from Barbara on how thoughtless he is. Earlier today, Barbara forgot to pick up Mitch's dry cleaning as she promised she would on the way home from work. Mitch was really upset. He told her how irresponsible she was, and slammed the door on his way out to the dry cleaners. He then stayed out for several hours. The excuse he used when he got back was that he was hungry and stopped for dinner, but it was clear that he was just angry with Barbara and wanted to teach her a lesson.

2. Jen and Jon are having a tough time around money. She wants to be able to take a vacation with the kids this year. Having gone over the budget, it is clear to her that they can afford it. Jon tends to be a very practical guy. He wants to stay home and just hang out together for their vacation, get some work done around the house, and maybe go to a local amusement park or something. When Jen says she wants to go on a vacation, Jon objects by saying that the household projects he wants to get done won't be accomplished if they go away. When Jon says he wants to work on the house, Jen accuses him of being a "stick-in-the-mud workaholic who wouldn't know how to have fun if it bit him on the rear end."

Discussion Questions

1. Considering what you learned from the video, what advice would you give Mitch and Barbara for getting their arguments under control?

2. Considering what you learned from the video, especially the information about negotiating the "how" and the "when" but not the "what," how would you advise Jen and Jon to resolve this conflict?

ACTIVITY

Heavenly Home Improvement Plan

1. Each day say yes to some need or reasonable request from your spouse that you tend to naturally want to say no to.

2. Each day recall your marital imperative and the virtues you identified as being central to your married life. Ask yourself, "How can I apply these virtues to the challenges I will face today, and what additional virtues might I need to practice as well?"

3. Keep up your daily individual and couple prayer time. Keep using the PRAISE format unless you have mutually decided to do something else. Continue to discuss your experience throughout the month, and make adjustments in your prayer time as necessary.

4. Keep looking for new ways to work together so that you can apply all the gifts of being a man or a woman to the problems, tasks, and challenges you face every day.

5. Work to become an expert in your mate's lovestyle.

6. And your new Heavenly Habit...

Practice taking your emotional temperature throughout the day. Find ways to take down your temperature before you open your mouth to discuss a complaint or a concern. When you do, practice using a clarifying question to assess the positive intention behind your mate's behavior. Use the Checkup Exercise in your workbook (see the following page) to keep track of your progress between now and the next time we meet.

Couples' Exercise:

- **Emotional Temperature Scale Exercise**

HEAVENLY HULLABALOO

EMOTIONAL TEMPERATURE SCALE EXERCISE

Each week review your use of the techniques discussed in this session on Heavenly Problem solving. For additional support, tips, and information, please see the chapter in *For Better...FOREVER!* titled "The Secrets of Red Hot Loving: How to Be Loving When Conflict Heats Things Up!"

1–3: Completely relaxed and peaceful.

4–5: Awake, alert, and attentive. Actively engaged in conversation and capable of effective problem solving.

6–7: Initial signs of adrenaline and cortisol build-up. Showing signs of non-verbal disgust and irritation. (Eye-rolling, heavy sighing, tsk-tsk-ing, refusal to look at one another when speaking, looking at your watch, etc.) TAKE A BREAK NOW!

7–8: Adrenaline and cortisol levels rapidly rising. Fight, flight, or freeze response initiated. You are expressing verbal disgust and irritation. The conversation is beginning to reflect less and less the mutual search for solutions and more and more the sense that your partner is the problem. You are losing the fight against the temptation to either begin lecturing your mate OR shut down on them as you continue the argument in your head. THIS IS THE POINT OF NO RETURN. YOU MUST BREAK NOW IF NOT BEFORE!

9–10: Adrenaline and cortisol flooding now at maximum levels. Problem-solving faculties are suspended as fight, flight, or freeze response is fully engaged. Everything you say or do at this point is either ordered to getting out of the conversation at all costs or overpowering your mate (verbally, emotionally, and/or physically) at all costs. You are powerless to do anything to stop it until the chemistry passes out of your system.

Week 1 _____

• Estimate your baseline emotional temperature as you go about your day.

_____

Note that if it is near 6+, you probably tend to feel like people are constantly trying to take advantage of you and/or you don't know how to effectively pace yourself. If your baseline temperature runs high, you have nowhere to go in conflict but crazy. Please identify some ways you plan to take down your emotional temperature in the coming weeks.

_____

_____

- What is your average emotional temperature in disagreements with your spouse? _____

Considering the suggestions in this session (and your reading of *For Better ...FOREVER!*), what strategies do you think would be helpful in keeping your temperature down?

- Give an example of a way you either assumed a positive intention, asked a clarifying question, or negotiated the How and the When but not the What this week.

_____

_____

- What will you do to improve on your effort in the coming weeks?

Week 2 _____

- Estimate your baseline emotional temperature as you go about your day.

_____

Note that if it is near 6+, you probably tend to feel like people are constantly trying to take advantage of you and/or you don't know how to effectively pace yourself. If your baseline temperature runs high, you have nowhere to go in conflict but crazy. Please identify some ways you plan to take down your emotional temperature this week.

_____

_____

- What is your average emotional temperature in disagreements with your spouse? _____

Considering the suggestions in this session (and your reading of *For Better ...FOREVER!*), what strategies do you think would be helpful in keeping your temperature down?

_____

_____

- Give an example of a way you either assumed a positive intention, asked a clarifying question, or negotiated the How and the When but not the What this week.

_____

_____

- What will you do to improve on your effort in the coming weeks?

_____

_____

Week 3 _____

- Estimate your baseline emotional temperature as you go about your day.

_____

Note that if it is near 6+, you probably tend to feel like people are constantly trying to take advantage of you and/or you don't know how to effectively pace yourself. If your baseline temperature runs high, you have nowhere to go in conflict but crazy. Please identify some ways you plan to take down your emotional temperature this week.

_____

_____

- What is your average emotional temperature in disagreements with your spouse? _____

Considering the suggestions in this session (and your reading of *For Better ...FOREVER!*), what strategies do you think would be helpful in keeping your temperature down?

_____

_____

- Give an example of a way you either assumed a positive intention, asked a clarifying question, or negotiated the How and the When but not the What this week.

_____

_____

- What will you do to improve on your effort in the coming weeks?

_____

_____

Week 4 _____

- Estimate your baseline emotional temperature as you go about your day.

_____

Note that if it is near 6+, you probably tend to feel like people are constantly trying to take advantage of you and/or you don't know how to effectively pace yourself. If your baseline temperature runs high, you have nowhere to go in conflict but crazy. Please identify some ways you plan to take down your emotional temperature this week.

_____

_____

- What is your average emotional temperature in disagreements with your spouse? _____

Considering the suggestions in this session (and your reading of *For Better ... FOREVER!*), what strategies do you think would be helpful in keeping your temperature down?

_____

_____

- Give an example of a way you either assumed a positive intention, asked a clarifying question, or negotiated the How and the When but not the What this week.

_____

_____

- What will you do to improve on your effort in the coming weeks?

_____

_____

HEAVENLY GRATITUDE

Never Feel Taken for Granted

❦ OPENING THE SESSION

Summary of Session Seven

Heavenly Couples know that their spouse is the greatest gift God will ever give them, second only to salvation and life. We need to be grateful for that gift. Everything our mate does for us — especially those things that we could do for ourselves — is an act of generosity and love that should be acknowledged as such in small but obvious ways. After all, if a mate isn't worth a compliment, a few words of thanks, some generous affection, or a token of our appreciation, how can that mate ever come to understand the immense bounty of love God has in store for him or her? Heavenly Gratitude enables couples to be Christ to one another by reflecting the ways God himself passionately cherishes each one of us. In this session, couples will discover simple habits they can cultivate to make sure neither is ever taken for granted and both can always feel grateful for each other.

Opening Prayer

Leader: Let's begin in the name of the Father and of the Son and of the Holy Spirit.

All: Amen.

Leader: Lord Jesus Christ, you have given our mate to us as our greatest treasure. But too often we treat the treasure you have entrusted to our care with disregard, callousness, and a lack of appreciation. You have asked us to be Christ to one another, to be the spouse that you would be. You never take us for granted. Though you are all-powerful, and we can do nothing without you, you shower us with grace and encouragement. For our smallest efforts, you promise a return of a hundred-fold. For our simple lives of meager service, you tell us, "Well done, my good and faithful servant!" To ransom a slave, you gave away your son. Teach us your ways, Lord God. Help us be profoundly grateful to our spouses for the simple acts of generosity, the small daily expressions of love and affection, the quiet acts of loving service, and most important, for the commitment to share a lifetime together.

We ask this through Christ our Lord.

All:	Amen.
Leader:	Let's take a moment to offer the prayers of our hearts to the Lord. We'll all pray together, "Lord, make us truly grateful."
Petition 1:	Lord, you have taught us through your saints that the secret to holiness is doing small things with great love. Help us to never stand in the way of our mate's holiness by treating their simple acts of loving service with disregard or disdain.
All:	Lord, make us truly grateful.
Petition 2:	Lord, the couples gathered here tonight have pledged their lives to one another. Help us always remember the awesome trust that is conveyed when one person places his life in another's hands.
All:	Lord, make us truly grateful.
Petition 3:	Lord, in the parable of the lost sheep, you remind us of how precious each one of us is to you. Help each husband and wife gathered here to always see each other as you see them — a precious gift to be valued, treasured, and praised.
All:	Lord, make us truly grateful
Leader:	If anyone would like to offer a petition of your own, please speak up now. (*Pause for petitions.*)
Leader:	Lord, you have given each husband and wife gathered here as a gift to each other. Help us to never take that gift for granted. Give us new eyes to see the loving acts of service and the generous ways our spouse makes our lives easier and more pleasant. Give us your words to thank and praise our spouse for those loving acts, and to thank and praise you for giving us such a treasured helpmate. We take a moment at this time to silently pray for the couple we have been praying for all these months. (*Moment of silence.*) We entrust our prayers to the intercession of your mother as we pray,
All:	Hail Mary . . . *Amen.*

Heavenly Witness

👓 VIDEO AND DISCUSSION

7

Question #1: How does gratitude help to insulate a marriage from conflict?

Question #2: How can gratitude serve as a catalyst for intimacy?

Question #3: Why is it important to overcome resistance to giving or receiving gratitude in a marriage?

👓 GROUP DISCUSSION EXERCISE

Case Study

Linda and Peter have been married for fourteen years. They have four children together. Linda works part-time while the children are in school. Peter works in sales at a local manufacturing company. They both say that their marriage is solid and that they love each other, but that something is missing.

"I don't think Peter knows how crazy my life can get sometimes," says Linda. "Sometimes, he'll just ask me to make some calls for him or pick something up, and I'd be happy to do it, but it isn't as if my day isn't packed already. Besides work, I have to pick up the kids after school, run them around to various activities, do most of the supervision of their homework, try to get some kind of dinner together . . . You name it. I'm going all the time. Peter's a good man, but I just don't think he really knows or appreciates everything I do and how much of it there is. And then he'll want to add something else to my plate, or he'll forget to do something I asked him to do, and he doesn't understand why I get upset. I swear, I love the man, but sometimes I want to wring his neck."

For his part, Peter says, "Linda can be pretty unforgiving at times. I have a very busy schedule all day, and sometimes I need her help, but when I ask her to do something that I just won't have time to do, she acts as if I'm asking her to carry the moon on her back. The other thing is, I spend a lot of time on the road all day and besides dealing with sales, I'm essentially the complaint department. If something doesn't go right, then I'm the guy my customers expect to fix it. It can be exhausting, and when I get home, sometimes I'm pretty drained. Then, when I walk in the door, without even saying 'Hello' or 'I love you,' she'll say, 'Hey Hon, I need to take a walk. Would you mind watching the kids? Oh, and dinner's in the oven. Take it out in 15 minutes, please.' And she's out the door. Look, I'm happy to give her some time to herself. I love spending time with the kids, and I actually like to cook more than she does. But I just don't feel like she has any appreciation for what my life is like."

Discussion Questions

1. If Linda and Peter increased their expressions of gratitude to one another, what differences do you think it would make in their lives?

2. What are the ways that Peter and Linda already make each other's lives easier or more pleasant? Are they currently experiencing these as acts of love or as entitlements?

3. Identify some simple ways that Peter and Linda could express their gratitude to one another.

🦋 ACTIVITY

Heavenly Home Improvement Plan

This month's Heavenly Habit is the following:

1. Make a list of all the things your spouse does throughout the day that benefit your marriage and family (e.g., going to work, cleaning the house, watching the kids, etc. Be specific).

2. Recognize that all of these things are tasks or simple acts of loving service that you would either have to do yourself or do without if you didn't have your mate.

3. List the ways you will demonstrate your gratitude to your spouse for doing these things. Examples include: saying "Thank you" when the particular task is performed, doing some extra act of service to make your mate's life easier or more pleasant, increasing the level of affection, or doing other things that your spouse has identified in earlier units that communicate love or appreciation. List them here.

Couples' Exercise:

· Heavenly Checkup

🦋 HEAVENLY HULLABALOO

HEAVENLY CHECKUP

Keep track of your progress with developing the Heavenly Habit of gratitude.

Week 1 _____

1. Generally speaking, how comfortable are you in expressing gratitude and appreciation?

> Extremely uncomfortable 1 2 3 4 5 6 7 8 9 10 Extremely comfortable

2. How successful do you think you were this week expressing gratitude and appreciation to your mate?

> Not at all successful 1 2 3 4 5 6 7 8 9 10 Totally successful

Give examples:

3. How successful do you think your mate was in expressing gratitude and appreciation to you?

> Not at all successful 1 2 3 4 5 6 7 8 9 10 Totally successful

Give examples of times that your mate's gratitude was especially appreciated.

Week 2 _____

1. Generally speaking, how comfortable are you in expressing gratitude and appreciation?

> Extremely uncomfortable 1 2 3 4 5 6 7 8 9 10 Extremely comfortable

Have you noticed any change from the previous week in your comfort level with expressing gratitude or appreciation? Y / N

2. How successful do you think you were this week expressing gratitude and appreciation to your mate?

> Not at all successful 1 2 3 4 5 6 7 8 9 10 Totally successful

Give examples:

3. How successful do you think your mate was in expressing gratitude and appreciation to you?

> Not at all successful 1 2 3 4 5 6 7 8 9 10 Totally successful

Give examples of times that your mate's gratitude was especially appreciated.

Week 3 _____

1. Generally speaking, how comfortable are you in expressing gratitude and appreciation?

> Extremely uncomfortable 1 2 3 4 5 6 7 8 9 10 Extremely comfortable

Have you noticed any change from the previous week in your comfort level with expressing gratitude or appreciation? Y / N

2. How successful do you think you were this week expressing gratitude and appreciation to your mate?

> Not at all successful 1 2 3 4 5 6 7 8 9 10 Totally successful

Give examples:

3. How successful do you think your mate was in expressing gratitude and appreciation to you?

> Not at all successful 1 2 3 4 5 6 7 8 9 10 Totally successful

Give examples of times that your mate's gratitude was especially appreciated.

Week 4

1. Generally speaking, how comfortable are you in expressing gratitude and appreciation?

> Extremely uncomfortable 1 2 3 4 5 6 7 8 9 10 Extremely comfortable

Have you noticed any change from the previous week in your comfort level with expressing gratitude or appreciation? Y / N

2. How successful do you think you were this week expressing gratitude and appreciation to your mate?

> Not at all successful 1 2 3 4 5 6 7 8 9 10 Totally successful

Give examples:

3. How successful do you think your mate was in expressing gratitude and appreciation to you?

> Not at all successful 1 2 3 4 5 6 7 8 9 10 Totally successful

Give examples of times that your mate's gratitude was especially appreciated.

HEAVENLY JOY

Celebrating Life and Love Together

8

OPENING THE SESSION

Summary of Session Eight

God rejoices in every moment his children spend with him. Similarly, couples must learn to cultivate and take joy in each other's presence. In this session, couples are invited to remember when they were first dating and the joy they experienced just being in each other's presence. In those days, it didn't matter what they were doing, as long as they were doing it together. In this session, couples are invited to rediscover this Heavenly Joy by learning to appreciate the truth, goodness, and beauty in all the things their mate finds true, good, and beautiful. In this way, one's spouse will always be one's best friend, the first person one thinks of to share both the celebrations and struggles of life.

Opening Prayer

Leader:	Let's begin in the name of the Father and of the Son and of the Holy Spirit.
All:	Amen.
Leader:	Lord Jesus Christ, you have told us that you came that we might have life and have it abundantly, and yet so many of our days are filled with drudgery, toil, and longer and longer lists of things to do. Help us to claim the gift of joy, that gift of your Holy Spirit given to all who have life in you. Help us to draw strength from our families to pursue the abundant life to which you call each of us — a life centered on meaningfulness, intimacy, and virtue. Help us take advantage of all the little ways we can celebrate your goodness in our homes and in our hearts.
	We ask this through Christ our Lord.
All:	Amen.
Leader:	Let's take a moment to offer the prayers of our hearts to the Lord. We'll all pray together, "Lord, give us the gift of joy."

Petition 1:	Lord, help us to appreciate the gift of life by finding ways to celebrate that gift as couples and families.
All:	Lord, give us the gift of joy.
Petition 2:	Lord, we are busy with many things. Help us to choose the better part by strengthening our relationships with you and with each other and experiencing the joy that comes from deepening those relationships.
All:	Lord, give us the gift of joy.
Petition 3:	Lord, you have asked us to become like little children. We who are weary and work-worn, teach us how to play.
All:	Lord, give us the gift of joy.
Leader:	If anyone would like to offer a petition of your own, please speak up now. (*Pause for petitions.*)
Leader:	Lord, we are gathered here tonight to learn about joy. Help us to learn many new ways to celebrate the gift of life and love you give to us every moment of every day. We take a moment at this time to silently pray for the couple we have been praying for all these months. (*Moment of silence.*) We entrust our prayers to the intercession of your mother as we pray,
All:	Hail Mary . . . *Amen.*

Heavenly Witness

☞ VIDEO AND DISCUSSION

Question #1: Why is joy important to marital and family life?

Question #2: What's the biggest threat to joy in marriage and family life?

Question #3: What's the importance of ritual and routine to the maintenance of joy?

 # GROUP DISCUSSION EXERCISE

Case Study

Gerilynn and Rob have been married twelve years and have three children, ages six through ten. Rob has his own business, and though he has regular office hours from eight to six Monday through Saturday, he tends to work whenever his clients need him. Gerilynn is very active in her children's school and in the church, where she participates in Catholic Women's Club as well as the Parent Teacher Organization and on the liturgy committee of the Parish Council. All of their children are involved in soccer as well as music lessons. It's not unusual for them to be going to one practice or another almost every night of the week. Weekends are usually taken up with their children's games or household chores.

"I know we're overcommitted," says Gerilynn, "but with the way Rob works it's not like we would be doing anything together with the family or as a couple anyway. I would hate to have the kids miss out on the chance to play sports or do their music. They really enjoy both, and I want to give them the chance to develop their full potential."

Rob, for his part, thinks things are fine the way they are. "Sure, we're busy, but what family isn't? We get along fine." When pressed, though, he admits, "Well, now that you mention it, Gerilynn and I don't have much of a sexual relationship. We're just too tired most of the time. As for prayer, we say grace and stuff, but not a lot more. And time to talk? I don't know. She'll usually call me on the cell when I'm at work to let me know where she's taking the kids, or if I have to fend for myself for dinner, and that sort of thing. But no, we don't talk much about where we're going as a family. Weekends, I usually have to take care of things like cutting the grass and different chores since I'm so busy during the week. That, or Gerilynn and I will end up running different kids to their games, so we don't really have any kind of family time on the weekends. Well, we do go to church together, but that's about it. We really don't spend much time together as a family, and come to think of it, I'm not sure the time we do spend together is all that enjoyable."

Discussion Questions

1. Do you think that Rob and Gerilynn are getting all they can out of their relationship? Are they teaching their children how to have close family relationships when they grow up? Explain your answer.

2. What suggestions could you make to Rob and Gerilynn for some rituals and routines that would help them get more out of their marriage?

3. Rob and Gerilynn and their children lead very busy lives. Suggest ideas for how they could make time for the suggestions you made in response to Question #2.

❧❧ ACTIVITY

Heavenly Home Improvement Plan

This month's Heavenly Habit is the following:

1. Discuss: What rituals and routines do you have as a couple that help nurture and maintain your joy? Do you feel that you're getting as much joy out of your marriage as you could?

2. If you'd like to get more joy out of your marriage, you will have to put more energy into establishing the rituals and routines that will support that goal. Look at the following areas and identify the additional activities (or activities you already practice but need to be more consistent about) that would increase your experience of togetherness and joy. (Focus on your marital relationship in this part of the exercise.)

Working Together:

Praying Together:

Talking Together:

Playing Together:

Sharing Affection Together:

3. Go back and review the categories listed under Question #2. What rituals or routines would you need to establish to increase the joy you experience in your whole family?

4. Sit down with your mate and schedule the activities you identified under Questions 2 and 3. Commit to making whatever changes you must make to enable these new rituals and routines to take hold. Remember, *activity* is less important than *relationship*. Joy does not come from doing, it comes from being together and sharing. To experience more joy in your marriage, you must break your addiction to doing and learn to be a community of persons, not a collection of individuals just living under the same roof.

Couples' Exercise:

• **Heavenly Checkup**

❦❦ HEAVENLY HULLABALOO

HEAVENLY CHECKUP

At the end of each week, evaluate your progress toward this Heavenly Habit. Discuss your answers with your spouse.

Week 1 _____

1. How effective were you at carving out time for your marriage this week?

    > Not at all effective 1 2 3 4 5 6 7 8 9 10 Totally effective

2. How effective were you at maintaining the rituals and routines you identified in this session?

    > Not at all effective 1 2 3 4 5 6 7 8 9 10 Totally effective

3. What, if anything, will you do this week to try to be more faithful to these rituals and routines or to build on the progress you have made so far?

Week 2 _____

1. How effective were you at carving out time for your marriage this week?

    > Not at all effective 1 2 3 4 5 6 7 8 9 10 Totally effective

2. How effective were you at maintaining the rituals and routines you identified in this session?

    > Not at all effective 1 2 3 4 5 6 7 8 9 10 Totally effective

3. What, if anything, will you do this week to try to be more faithful to these rituals and routines or to build on the progress you have made so far?

Week 3 _____

1. How effective were you at carving out time for your marriage this week?

   > Not at all effective 1 2 3 4 5 6 7 8 9 10 Totally effective

2. How effective were you at maintaining the rituals and routines you identified in this session?

   > Not at all effective 1 2 3 4 5 6 7 8 9 10 Totally effective

3. What, if anything, will you do this week to try to be more faithful to these rituals and routines or to build on the progress you have made so far?

Week 4 _____

1. How effective were you at carving out time for your marriage this week?

   > Not at all effective 1 2 3 4 5 6 7 8 9 10 Totally effective

2. How effective were you at maintaining the rituals and routines you identified in this session?

   > Not at all effective 1 2 3 4 5 6 7 8 9 10 Totally effective

3. What, if anything, will you do this week to try to be more faithful to these rituals and routines or to build on the progress you have made so far?

9

HEAVENLY FIDELITY

Getting Your Priorities in Order

❧❧ OPENING THE SESSION

Summary of Session Nine

Heavenly Fidelity involves more than avoiding physical intimacy outside of marriage. It refers to a couple's ability to set appropriate limits on all those relationships that compete with the primacy of the marital relationship (work, friends, other commitments). Because marriage is the relationship in which the couple's Christian identity is being most actively formed, this relationship has a right to the lion's share of the couple's time, attention, and energy. Failing to live exceptional fidelity jeopardizes the likelihood that the couple will become the people God created them to be since it most likely means that they are choosing activity over intimacy and stress over sanctification. Participating couples are given a simple but practical tool for determining how much time their marriage and family life requires to function well and how to secure this time and energy.

Opening Prayer

Leader: Let's begin in the name of the Father and of the Son and of the Holy Spirit.

All: Amen.

Leader: Lord Jesus Christ, you are always faithful to us. Help us to remember that in spite of the many things that compete for our attentions and distract us, nothing is more important than becoming the people you created us to be and preparing to become one with you in the Eternal Wedding Feast. Help us to dedicate ourselves to making our homes into communities of love that challenge and inspire us to pursue perfection in Christ first and foremost.

We ask this through Christ our Lord.

All: Amen.

Leader:	Let's take a moment to offer the prayers of our hearts to the Lord. We'll all pray together, "Lord, make us faithful as you are faithful."
Petition 1:	Lord, there are so many things to do. Help us to never forget that the most important thing is to make time to love the people you have given us to care for and to take care of us.
All:	Lord, make us faithful as you are faithful.
Petition 2:	Lord, our minds are full of so many worries, thoughts, ideas, and desires. Help us to be always mindful of our vocation of marriage and always faithful to our commitment to place each other first above all other commitments and relationships.
All:	Lord, make us faithful as you are faithful.
Petition 3:	Lord, everyone says that their marriage comes first. Help our lives to truly reflect those words.
All:	Lord, make us faithful as you are faithful.
Leader:	If anyone would like to offer a petition of your own, please speak up now. (*Pause for petitions.*)
Leader:	Lord, we are gathered here tonight to learn about Heavenly Fidelity. Help us to learn many new ways to celebrate the gifts of life and love that you give to us every moment of every day. We take a moment at this time to silently pray for the couple we have been praying for all these months. (*Moment of silence.*) We entrust our prayers to the intercession of your mother as we pray,
All:	Hail Mary . . . *Amen.*

Heavenly Witness

🐦🐦 VIDEO AND DISCUSSION

Question #1: What does our commitment to fidelity in marriage really require of us?

Question #2: What is the personal benefit of living Heavenly Fidelity in marriage?

Question #3: What is the formula we can use to identify how much time and energy our family requires to help each member become the people God is calling us to be?

GROUP DISCUSSION EXERCISE

Case Study

Armeda and Juan have been married fifteen years. They have three children, ages six, nine, and twelve. Armeda is employed as a phlebotomist at the local hospital, and Juan is a manager at a major department store. In addition to their full-time jobs, both are active in their parish and community. Armeda is a lector in her parish and helps distribute communion to shut-ins. She also volunteers some time each week at the local animal shelter. Juan is active on parish council and is a coach for their two sons' Little League teams as well as being involved in the Knights of Columbus. All their children take karate as well, and their daughter is involved in dance classes twice a week.

Added to this mix, Armeda's thirty-seven-year-old brother is a recovering alcoholic who lives with her parents, who are getting on in years. Regularly, her parents call her to complain about her brother, or to seek help with his care, or to transport him to his AA meetings, since he lost his license after being convicted of a DUI and being court-ordered to treatment.

Lately, Armeda and Juan have been feeling more distant from each other. "I can't remember the last time we had a date," says Armeda, "and our sexual relationship has gotten completely squeezed out."

Juan agrees. "With everything going on with work, Armeda's family, and the kids, we pretty much fall into bed at the end of the day just glad we survived. We don't have a lot of time for the things we used to do. Our prayer time as a family is basically limited to grace at meals. We used to do a game night, and Sunday was always our family day. But lately, with baseball games and dance competitions, the family is always going in a million different directions, and Armeda and I rarely get any time together at all."

Armeda and Juan are frustrated and feel that they're being pulled apart. "But," says Armeda, "I don't know any other family that is doing any better than we are. When we look around, it seems like everyone lives like this. I wish it didn't have to be this way, but I don't know any way out."

Discussion Questions

1. How could the concept of Heavenly Fidelity help Armeda and Juan find a healthier balance in their lives?

2. If Armeda and Juan were to use the formula described in the video, what are some of the family and marriage activities they might need to make a commitment to restarting?

3. Heavenly Fidelity requires us to sometimes decline invitations to do certain things for others or join certain activities because they would take a disproportionate amount of our time and threaten the primacy of our marriage and family life. Even so, it can be difficult to say no even when we know we should. Think of some times that you have successfully withdrawn from an activity or placed limits on a relationship that was taking too much of your time. Describe what you think is the best way to practice the skill of saying no when the circumstances require it.

🕊️🕊️ ACTIVITY

9

Heavenly Home Improvement Plan

This month's Heavenly Habit is the following:

Do the Heavenly Fidelity formula described in the video. Use the steps in the Heavenly Fidelity Exercise on the following page. Also do the Heavenly Checkup (page 90) to reflect on your effectiveness in following these steps.

Couples' Exercise:

- **Heavenly Fidelity Exercise**
- **Heavenly Checkup**

🕊️🕊️ HEAVENLY HULLABALOO

HEAVENLY FIDELITY EXERCISE

1. Think of a week in which each member of your family — especially you and your spouse — have felt closer to one another than usual. Identify the kinds of rituals, routines, and activities you engaged in that week that brought you closer together (e.g., prayer/praise time, date night, game night, family day, family meals, and other activities that you as a couple or family enjoy). Estimate the number of hours you spent together relating to each other in these kinds of activities. Use the following chart:

Activity   Time Spent in Activity
                                                                         Each Week

_____   _____

_____   _____

_____   _____

_____   _____

_____   _____

_____   _____

_____   _____

_____   _____

Add the "Time Spent" column for TOTAL TIME   _____

This total represents a thumbnail sketch of the number of hours your marriage and family requires to function well. The activities on the left represent some of the kinds of things you can do with that time to get the best results, but there are probably other things you could also do.

2. Each week sit down together with your calendars and carve out the amount of time that you identified your marriage/family needs to function well.

3. Some weeks emergencies may occur, and it may not be possible to get all your marriage and family time in. This, however, *must* be the exception to the rule. Remember that on those weeks that it is not possible to spend this much time together, you are — metaphorically

speaking — "borrowing" time for other activities from your "marriage and family bank." You will have to make certain to put the amount of time you take from your marriage and family back into the "account" in subsequent weeks, or your account will become overdrawn, and the rapport you experience in your home will collapse.

4. Looking at the amount of time your marriage and family need to function well, how do you think you'll need to restructure work and other activities to accommodate your commitment to Heavenly Fidelity? What specific information will you need to seek out, or what steps will you need to take, to make this transition possible? What do you think will be the easiest changes to make or the simplest conflicts to resolve? What will be the most difficult changes?

5. If making some of these changes seems overwhelming, go easy on yourself. Take small steps, and make one change at a time. Work together over the next several months to make the changes necessary to schedule, and jealously guard, the amount of time your marriage and family need to become all that God wants it to be.

🕊️ HEAVENLY CHECKUP

At the end of each week, evaluate your progress toward this Heavenly Habit. Discuss your answers with your spouse.

Week 1 _____

1. How effective were you at carving out time for your marriage this week?

Not at all effective 1 2 3 4 5 6 7 8 9 10 Totally effective

2. How effective were you at maintaining the rituals and routines you identified in this session?

Not at all effective 1 2 3 4 5 6 7 8 9 10 Totally effective

3. What, if anything, will you do this week to try to be more faithful to these rituals and routines or to build on the progress you've made so far?

Week 2 _____

1. How effective were you at carving out time for your marriage this week?

Not at all effective 1 2 3 4 5 6 7 8 9 10 Totally effective

2. How effective were you at maintaining the rituals and routines you identified in this session?

Not at all effective 1 2 3 4 5 6 7 8 9 10 Totally effective

3. What, if anything, will you do this week to try to be more faithful to these rituals and routines or to build on the progress you've made so far?

Week 3 _____

1. How effective were you at carving out time for your marriage this week?

> Not at all effective 1 2 3 4 5 6 7 8 9 10 Totally effective

2. How effective were you at maintaining the rituals and routines you identified in this session?

> Not at all effective 1 2 3 4 5 6 7 8 9 10 Totally effective

3. What, if anything, will you do this week to try to be more faithful to these rituals and routines or to build on the progress you've made so far?

Week 4 _____

1. How effective were you at carving out time for your marriage this week?

> Not at all effective 1 2 3 4 5 6 7 8 9 10 Totally effective

2. How effective were you at maintaining the rituals and routines you identified in this session?

> Not at all effective 1 2 3 4 5 6 7 8 9 10 Totally effective

3. What, if anything, will you do this week to try to be more faithful to these rituals and routines or to build on the progress you've made so far?

10

HEAVENLY FAMILY

Life and Love after Kids

🎀 OPENING THE SESSION

Summary of Session Ten

Contemporary society teaches couples that children are a threat to intimacy. This session explores the gift that children are to a couple and how a couple can grow closer together because of their children rather than in spite of them. The church teaches that couples are to preside over "schools of love." That is, they are called to create a family environment that models authentic love and true intimacy. In this session, couples are taught to find ways to express love and romance all day long, every day (as opposed to just saving expressions of love for "date night" when the children aren't around) so that they can stay connected and model healthy relationships to their children.

Opening Prayer

Leader:	Let's begin in the name of the Father and of the Son and of the Holy Spirit.
All:	Amen.
Leader:	Lord Jesus Christ, the love that you share with the Father and Holy Spirit overflows to us, your children, and calls us and all of creation into greater union with you, leading to a continuing, ever-expanding circle of unity and creativity. You created the human family in the image of the Trinity, so that as a husband and wife shared their love for one another, their love would bring forth children who would in turn draw the couple closer together in an ever-expanding circle of unity and procreativity. Help us to experience our children as a gift. Help us to learn to love each other more *because of* our children rather than in spite of our children. Strengthen our families, so that we might become the communities of love that we are called to be.
	We ask this through Christ our Lord.

All:	Amen.
Leader:	Let's take a moment to offer the prayers of our hearts to the Lord. We'll all pray together, "Lord, make us a family of love."
Petition 1:	Lord, sometimes we can feel that our own children are a threat to the intimacy we share as husband and wife. Expand our capacity for love, and help us to always have the time and energy to love both our children and each other fully, totally, and completely.
All:	Lord, make us a family of love.
Petition 2:	Lord, on the day that we wed, we promised to love one another with a love that is free, faithful, forever, and *fruitful*. Help us to be open to receiving the children you wish to give us — by birth or adoption — and help us to exercise both the prudence and generosity that are essential for responsible parenthood.
All:	Lord, make us a family of love.
Petition 3:	Lord, help us to love our spouse and our children with *your* love, so that our well may never run dry, and that each member of our family can feel that he or she is cherished, treasured, and loved abundantly.
All:	Lord, make us a family of love.
Leader:	If anyone would like to offer a petition of your own, please speak up now. (*Pause for petitions.*)
Leader:	Lord, we are gathered here tonight to learn about becoming a Heavenly Family. Help us to share more fully in the gift of your abundant love that our families would be a source of joy and strength for all those within our home, and a source of hope and inspiration for all those who dwell outside our home. We take a moment at this time to silently pray for the couple we have been praying for all these months. (*Moment of silence.*) We entrust our prayers to the intercession of your mother as we pray,
All:	Hail Mary . . . *Amen.*

Heavenly Witness

🐦🐦 VIDEO AND DISCUSSION

10

Presentation of Focus Questions

Question #1: What is God's plan for families, and how can children actually increase the intimacy in marriage?

Question #2: What is the major transition that occurs once a couple has children, and how can a couple successfully negotiate that transition?

Question #3: What is the most important attitude to have toward love and romance once children come on the scene?

🐦🐦 GROUP DISCUSSION EXERCISE

Case Study

Martin and Sara have been married fifteen years. They have four children. With the birth of their last child (now three years old), it felt to Martin and Sara that the problems in their relationship had reached critical mass.

Sara explains, "I just don't have any energy left. Between my part-time job and taking care of the lion's share of the kids and the house, I just feel like I've got nothing left."

Martin responds, "Ever since we started having kids, Sara has less and less energy for me. I tell her we need to get out more, but we don't have anyone to watch the kids, and she won't find anybody. Any time I ask about maybe getting some time to make love, she treats me like I ought to file a request in triplicate with the home office. I love the kids and all, but I'm getting a little sick of getting the dregs of my wife."

Sara has heard this before. "I just think that once you get married and start having kids, things change. Martin's a big boy. He can take care of himself. Honest to God, sometimes I feel like I have five kids instead of four."

"What do you mean!" exclaims Martin. "I help with the dishes! I clean up! I help out all the time!"

"Yes, you do," says Sara, "but usually I have to ask. And then, you don't always finish. I have to check up afterward to see that everything got done. As for sex, I think you've got some crazy idea that I'm supposed to be able to go from washing the dishes to wiping the little one's nose, to swinging from the chandelier with you. I've got a news flash for you, babe. I love you, but that isn't ever going to happen."

Martin sighs. "It wasn't like this before kids. I love my kids, but if I had to do it over again, I would have done it very differently."

Discussion Questions

1. What do you think about Martin and Sara's attitude to marriage with children? Does romance really have to go on life support for the sake of the children?

2. Considering tonight's video presentation, if you were in a position to give advice to Martin and Sara about how to turn their relationship around, what would you suggest? In particular, what suggestions would you make to help them take better advantage of their day-to-day relationship instead of waiting and hoping for date night?

 # ACTIVITY

Heavenly Home Improvement Plan

This month's Heavenly Habit is as follows:

1. Complete the Lovelist Exercise.

2. Practice the Marital Examination of Conscience.

3. Use the Heavenly Checkup to evaluate your progress with the previous two exercises.

Couples' Exercises:

- **Lovelist Exercise**
- **Marital Examination of Conscience**
- **Heavenly Checkup**

⌘ HEAVENLY HULLABALOO

LOVELIST EXERCISE

Directions: Identify at least twenty-five things that make you feel loved or special or make your day easier or more pleasant when they are done for you. The items should not involve a great deal of time, effort, or expense. Be specific and positive. This is not a complaint list. After completing the exercise, exchange your lists with each other. Assuming that you are not being asked to do anything that is immoral or demeaning, make a commitment to do at least one or two of the items your partner identified on his or her list. Be prepared to discuss what you did in your nightly Marital Examination of Conscience (see the following page).

Twenty-five Things...

_____   _____

_____   _____

_____   _____

_____   _____

_____   _____

_____   _____

_____   _____

_____   _____

_____   _____

_____   _____

_____   _____

_____   _____

_____

This list is meant to inspire other creative ideas. Use this as a springboard for exploring even more ways to be loving to each other!

MARITAL EXAMINATION OF CONSCIENCE

Directions: First, take some time for prayer together. We suggest using the PRAISE format discussed on page 28. Then discuss the following:

1. What little things did you do today to try to make each other's day easier or more pleasant?

2. Are there any kinds of special encouragement or support that you would appreciate from each other tomorrow? What specifically would you like your spouse to do to express that support?

3. Do you feel that you're getting the most out of your Lovelist? Is there something you would like to add or change about your Lovelist?

Close with a brief prayer. For instance,
> *Lord Jesus Christ.*
> *Thank you for my (husband/wife). Help me to love (him or her) better each day, so that (he or she) always knows what a precious gift (he or she) is.*
> *Amen.*

♥♥ HEAVENLY CHECKUP

At the end of each week, evaluate your progress toward this Heavenly Habit. Discuss your answers with your spouse.

Week 1 _____

1. How effective were you applying your Lovelist Exercise this week?

   > Not at all effective 1 2 3 4 5 6 7 8 9 10 Totally effective

2. How effective were you at practicing the Marital Examination of Conscience this week?

   > Not at all effective 1 2 3 4 5 6 7 8 9 10 Totally effective

3. What, if anything, will you do this week to try to be more faithful to these rituals and routines or to build on the progress you have made so far?

Week 2 _____

1. How effective were you applying your Lovelist Exercise this week?

   > Not at all effective 1 2 3 4 5 6 7 8 9 10 Totally effective

2. How effective were you at practicing the Marital Examination of Conscience this week?

   > Not at all effective 1 2 3 4 5 6 7 8 9 10 Totally effective

3. What, if anything, will you do this week to try to be more faithful to these rituals and routines or to build on the progress you have made so far?

Week 3 _____

1. How effective were you applying your Lovelist Exercise this week?

> Not at all effective 1 2 3 4 5 6 7 8 9 10 Totally effective

2. How effective were you at practicing the Marital Examination of Conscience this week?

> Not at all effective 1 2 3 4 5 6 7 8 9 10 Totally effective

3. What, if anything, will you do this week to try to be more faithful to these rituals and routines or to build on the progress you have made so far?

Week 4 _____

1. How effective were you applying your Lovelist Exercise this week?

> Not at all effective 1 2 3 4 5 6 7 8 9 10 Totally effective

2. How effective were you at practicing the Marital Examination of Conscience this week?

> Not at all effective 1 2 3 4 5 6 7 8 9 10 Totally effective

3. What, if anything, will you do this week to try to be more faithful to these rituals and routines or to build on the progress you have made so far?

11

HEAVENLY SEX

The Secrets of Soulful Loving

🎀 OPENING THE SESSION

Summary of Session Eleven

While some couples think of sex as recreation, Heavenly Couples recognize that lovemaking is a re-creation of their wedding day and a renewal of their wedding vows spoken in a profound, physical language of love that transcends words. Heavenly Couples know how to love with their whole selves, their bodies, minds, and souls, and they know how to see their lovemaking as a prayer that physically manifests God's love for each of them. Finally, Heavenly Couples know how to celebrate the sanctifying power of sex by living all the virtues connected to the unity and creativity of their marriage and by being well-versed in the spiritual and practical dimensions of Natural Family Planning.

Opening Prayer

Leader: Let's begin in the name of the Father and of the Son and of the Holy Spirit.

All: Amen.

Leader: Lord Jesus Christ, you gave us sexuality as your gift to humankind that men and women might have the means of experiencing with their whole being, the passionate love you hold in your heart for each and every one of us. Give each couple gathered here the grace to be physical signs of your love. We give you our sexuality, and we ask you, God, Author of both love and passion, to teach each couple gathered here tonight how to be truly godly and soulful lovers to one another. Help us to reject the false messages in our culture that seek to deface the blessing of sexuality and empower us to celebrate the eternal truth, unfathomable beauty, and profound goodness of Christian marital love.

	We ask this through Christ our Lord.
All:	Amen.
Leader:	Let's take a moment to offer the prayers of our hearts to the Lord. We'll all pray together, "Lord, teach us how to love."
Petition 1:	Lord, it is your intention that sex would be a physical sign of the spiritual and emotional unity that exists between husband and wife. Help us that we might never pretend to speak unity with our bodies while speaking disunity with our lives.
All:	Lord, teach us how to love.
Petition 2:	Lord, it is so easy to treat sex as a means to an end, using it to please ourselves at the expense of each other and our relationship. Give us your grace. Help us to always use our sexuality in ways that convey our respect, our love, and our desire to serve one another with our whole heart, mind, soul, and body.
All:	Lord, teach us how to love.
Petition 3:	Lord, help us to see sex, not just as recreation, but as a re-creation of our wedding day in which we are given the grace to renew our commitment to love each other in a language that transcends words.
All:	Lord, teach us how to love.
Leader:	If anyone would like to offer a petition of your own, please speak up now. (*Pause for petitions.*)
Leader:	Lord, the temptation is strong to close you out of significant parts of our lives. It is too easy to give you only the aspects of ourselves we are comfortable with. Today, Lord, we recommit ourselves to giving you every part of our lives and relationships, including the most intimate part, our sexuality. You created sex so that husband and wife could be physical signs of *your* passionate love for each of us, and so that we could share in the joy you take in bringing new life into the world to love and be loved by. Teach us to be the lovers you intended us to be when you called us together in marriage, so that we might experience the abundant, passionate, fulfilling, and grace-filled love you intended for us when you called us together in marriage. We take a moment at this time to silently pray for the couple we have been praying for

all these months. (*Moment of silence.*) We ask all this through the intercession of our Mother....

All: Hail Mary ... *Amen.*

11

Heavenly Witness

❦❦ **VIDEO AND DISCUSSION**

Question #1:   Does the church teach that Catholic couples should be suspicious of their sexuality? What does it mean to say, "sex is holy"?

Question #2:   What are the four paths to Sacred Sex?

Question #3:   What roles does prayer play in the development of a healthy sexuality between a husband and wife?

Four Paths to Sacred Sex

1. Guard each other's dignity.

2. Approach each other joyfully.

3. Approach each other in prayer.

4. Maintain a responsible openness to life.

❦❦ GROUP DISCUSSION EXERCISE

Case Study

Robert and Alison have been married for twelve years. They have three children. They attend Mass weekly and are both catechists in the Parish School of Religion. Robert works in administration at a local manufacturing company. Allison is a computer programmer. Lately, they've been struggling because of tension over their sexual relationship.

Robert is frustrated because the frequency of their lovemaking has dropped considerably in the last few years.

"I just feel like our sexual relationship gets short shrift all the time. I try to ask, but she just isn't interested."

Alison respond, "Look, we're not kids anymore. I love him, but I'm tired at the end of the day, and frankly, I feel like he pretty much ignores me unless he wants to have sex. Then, all of a sudden, he brings home some flowers and he expects me to be raring to go."

Robert says, "The only time she was really into it was when we were having kids. Don't get me wrong, I love our kids, but I felt like all she wanted out of me was babies. Then, when she got what she wanted, she was done with me."

"That's ridiculous," says Alison. "I enjoy sex as much as the next woman. I would like to have more kids, but Robert just keeps saying, 'no way.' I mean, I know that we already have more kids than most people, but I just don't feel like I'm ready to be done being a mom."

Robert glares. "I'm just waiting for you to start being a wife."

Asked how much their strong faith informs their attitudes toward their sexual relationship, Robert and Alison both roll their eyes. This is one thing they can both agree on. Alison says, "I think the church is really very backward about sex. Look, I'm sorry, but I'm not sure what a bunch of old, celibate men can possibly know about sex."

Robert adds, "I love my faith, but as far as sex and the church go, it's all about guilt. The Church is totally in the dark ages about sex. Other than telling us that we should have, like, four hundred kids or something, I really don't think there's anything the church can tell us about sex that we don't already know."

Discussion Questions

1. Robert's and Alison's opinions are certainly common enough. Considering what you learned in tonight's presentation, are their perceptions of the church's teaching on sexuality accurate? Why or why not?

2. Drawing primarily from the advice you heard in this session, what suggestions might you give Robert and Alison that might help them begin to work through some of their sexual concerns?

🐝 ACTIVITY

Heavenly Home Improvement Plan

This month's Heavenly Habit is the following:

1. Work on the spiritual aspects of your sexual relationship. Develop a Lover's Prayer and ask God to help both of you learn to love each other with his love. Also, get in the habit of praying together each day about whether God is calling you to respond better in some way (temporally, emotionally, or spiritually) to the family you already have, or if God is telling you it's time to consider adding another member to your family.

2. Contact one of the following organizations to learn more about Natural Family Planning. Even if you are not convinced that NFP is for you, information never hurt anyone. In fact, this really is one instance where what you don't know can hurt you. Take a moment to evaluate the facts, not just what you've heard.

   - The Couple to Couple League: *www.ccli.org*

   - The Pope Paul VI Institute: *www.popepaulvi.com*

   - The United States Catholic Conference of Bishops Natural Family Planning Office: *www.usccb.org/prolife/issues/nfp/*

3. Use the Heavenly Checkup see the following page to evaluate your progress toward Heavenly Sex.

Couples' Exercise:

- Heavenly Checkup

♥♥ HEAVENLY HULLABALOO

HEAVENLY CHECKUP

At the end of each week, evaluate your progress toward this Heavenly Habit. Discuss your answers with your spouse.

Week 1 _____

1. How effective were you with bringing God into your sexual life (i.e., developing and praying a Lover's Prayer, praying to discern God's will for your family size)?

> Not at all effective 1 2 3 4 5 6 7 8 9 10 Totally effective

2. How effective were you at finding out information and discussing your thoughts about Natural Family Planning?

> Not at all effective 1 2 3 4 5 6 7 8 9 10 Totally effective

3. What, if anything, will you do this week to try to be more attentive to these habits or to build on the progress you have made so far?

Week 2 _____

1. How effective were you with bringing God into your sexual life (i.e., developing and praying a Lover's Prayer, praying to discern God's will for your family size)?

> Not at all effective 1 2 3 4 5 6 7 8 9 10 Totally effective

2. How effective were you at finding out information and discussing your thoughts about Natural Family Planning?

> Not at all effective 1 2 3 4 5 6 7 8 9 10 Totally effective

3. What, if anything, will you do this week to try to be more attentive to these habits or to build on the progress you have made so far?

Week 3 _____

1. How effective were you with bringing God into your sexual life (i.e., developing and praying a Lover's Prayer, praying to discern God's will for your family size)?

> Not at all effective 1 2 3 4 5 6 7 8 9 10 Totally effective

2. How effective were you at finding out information and discussing your thoughts about Natural Family Planning?

> Not at all effective 1 2 3 4 5 6 7 8 9 10 Totally effective

3. What, if anything, will you do this week to try to be more attentive to these habits or to build on the progress you have made so far?

Week 4 _____

1. How effective were you with bringing God into your sexual life (i.e., developing and praying a Lover's Prayer, praying to discern God's will for your family size)?

> Not at all effective 1 2 3 4 5 6 7 8 9 10 Totally effective

2. How effective were you at finding out information and discussing your thoughts about Natural Family Planning?

> Not at all effective 1 2 3 4 5 6 7 8 9 10 Totally effective

3. What, if anything, will you do this week to try to be more attentive to these habits or to build on the progress you have made so far?

12

HEAVENLY COUPLEHOOD

Witnessing to the Power of Love

❧❧ OPENING THE SESSION

Summary of Session Twelve

The year culminates in a ceremony in which the couples who participated in the entire program earn their "wings." Participating couples renew their wedding vows and commit to continue to grow in their understanding of what it means to be a Heavenly Couple. They will receive a certificate of completion from their spouse. On that certificate are their wings, along with a space for the couples to write special words to each other. The wings symbolize their commitment and are blessed during the ceremony so that the couples can pin each other following their renewal of vows.

Couples who complete the one-year experience are encouraged to repeat the program. With each year, the couples' understanding of the material increases. Likewise, Heavenly Couples who have completed the entire program can share their wisdom with neophyte Heavenly Marriage enrollees and are encouraged to become sponsor couples to the newly engaged and newly married.

Opening Prayer

Leader: Let's begin in the name of the Father and of the Son and of the Holy Spirit.

All: Amen.

Leader: Lord Jesus Christ, you have given us marriage as a gift to help us learn how to love and to prepare us to spend an eternity loving you. Help us to always remember the heavenly purpose of our marriage in all that we do. Help us to remember that, by taking care of our marriage and each other, we are not only doing the work necessary to have a good earthly marriage, but we are learning to be the loving, generous, self-giving people you need us to be. Renew our hearts and our homes so that the love we share can be a beacon that draws the world closer to you.

	We ask this through Christ our Lord.
All:	Amen.
Leader:	Let's take a moment to offer the prayers of our hearts to the Lord. We'll all pray together, "Lord, teach us how to love."
Petition 1:	Lord, in the challenges of everyday married life, help us to always call on you for guidance and strength.
All:	Lord, teach us how to love.
Petition 2:	Lord, in the difficulties we face as Christian married couples, help us to cling to the habits we have been striving to cultivate over the last year. Let us continue to seek new ways to nurture our marriage and always remain faithful to our commitment to grow in our relationships with you and with one another.
All:	Lord, teach us how to love.
Petition 3:	Lord, so many things compete for our attention. Help us to always place our marriage and family life first, so that our spouse and children always get the best of us — not what's left of us.
All:	Lord, teach us how to love.
Leader:	If anyone would like to offer a petition of your own, please speak up now. (*Pause for petitions.*)
Leader:	Lord, the world is a hostile place for marriage and family life. Strengthen us that we might resist those temptations that would endanger our marriages. Fill us with your love that we might always remember that we do not love each other on our own power, but with your grace. Help us to be the partner you want us to be, the partner you would be to our mate. We take a final moment to pray silently for the couple we have been praying for these past months. (*Moment of silence.*) We ask all this through the intercession of our Mother....
All:	Hail Mary ... *Amen.*

Heavenly Witness
Video Presentation

RECOMMITMENT CEREMONY

12

Reader: A Reading from the Song of Songs (Song of Songs 2:8–17)

Responsorial Psalm

Gospel: Wedding Feast of Cana (John 2:1–11)

Homily

Celebrant: Lord, these couples have committed themselves to learning and living out your plan for marriage. Help them continue to live out their commitment to love, draw them closer to you and to each other, and give them the grace to stand as signs of your love for the world.

All: Amen.

Celebrant: God has given us the command to be perfect as his Heavenly Father is perfect — perfect in love. Let us call upon the Author of Love, that he might instruct our hearts to live in his perfect love for one another. We will respond to these petitions by praying, "Lord, make us steadfast in love."

Reader or Celebrant:

That the couples gathered here would continue their commitment to living out the message of the *Marriage Made for Heaven* program, and that they would continue to challenge themselves to love each other as God loves them.

All: Lord, make us steadfast in love.

Reader or Celebrant:

That the couples gathered here would live lives of generous love, giving to each other not only what they want to give, but also what they need to give to help each other become the people God created them to be.

All: Lord, make us steadfast in love.

Reader or Celebrant:

That every part of our lives, especially our romantic lives and physical intimacy, would be open to receiving God's grace, so that every couple here could truly be physical signs of God's love for each of them.

All: Lord, make us steadfast in love.

Reader or Celebrant:

That you would strengthen these couples here today that they can always find the resolve to give each other the first fruits of their love, time, and energy.

All: Lord, make us steadfast in love.

Reader or Celebrant:

That the couples gathered here would always remember that the most important work of their marriage is to help each other become the people you created them to be, and to help each other arrive properly attired for the Eternal Wedding Feast.

All: Lord, make us steadfast in love.

Celebrant: O God, hear our prayers, and grant each of the couples gathered here the grace to imitate the Holy Family that they might praise you and bear witness to your glory by living the fullness of your plan for marriage. We ask this through Christ our Lord.

All: Amen.

Celebrant: (*Omit if priest or deacon is unavailable*) I would ask the couples to come forward, bow your heads, and pray for God's blessing.

Couples come forward and stand before the celebrant.

Celebrant: Blessed are you, O Lord our God, King of the Universe. In the beginning, it pleased you to create man and woman and invite them to share in celebrating and revealing the power of your love to the world.

Celebrant: + Bless these couples gathered here today. Look with kindness and mercy upon them as they strive to live the fullness of married love. May they be a beacon of light in a dark world that is hungry for the witness of godly love. Strengthen them through difficult times, grant them many joys, sustain the covenant of love between them through all their days, and give them many happy, grace-filled years together, surrounded by the blessed presence of their children and their children's children. We ask this through Christ our Lord.

All: Amen.

🦋 HEAVENLY HULLABALOO

HEAVENLY HOME IMPROVEMENT PLAN

1. Each day say yes to some need or reasonable request from your spouse that you tend to naturally want to say no to.

2. Each day recall your marital imperative and the virtues you identified as being central to your married life. Ask yourself, "How can I apply these virtues to the challenges I will face today, and what additional virtues might I need to practice as well?"

3. Keep up your daily individual and couple prayer time. Keep using the PRAISE format unless you have mutually decided to do something else. Continue to discuss your experience throughout the month, and make adjustments in your prayer time as necessary.

4. Keep looking for new ways to work together so that you can apply all the gifts of being a man or a woman to the problems, tasks, and challenges you face every day.

5. Work to become an expert in your mate's lovestyle.

6. Practice taking your emotional temperature throughout the day. Find ways to take down your temperature before you open your mouth to discuss a complaint or a concern. When you do, practice using a clarifying question to assess the positive intention behind your mate's behavior.

7. Remember that everything your spouse does for you that you could, conceivably, do for yourself is an act of love. Make sure to look for ways to express your gratitude for these generous acts of service.

8. Be mindful of the rituals and routines that help you draw closer in every aspect of your relationship (work, prayer, communication, play). Work to protect those rituals.

9. Be mindful of the amount of time you need as a couple each week to feel good about each other and your relationship. Make a point of planning (and writing on your schedule) how you will make that time happen this week.

10. Stay connected every day by doing at least two things on your mate's Lovelist (one easy and one that's a little more challenging). Do your

"Marital Examination of Conscience" each evening to evaluate how well you attended to the marriage that day and to identify new ways to serve each other.

11. Pray your "Lover's Prayer" daily to ask God to teach you to be the loving, sensitive, passionate lover he wants you to be. Also, maintain a responsible openness to life by making sure that every month you spend some time talking and praying together about God's plan for your family size and overcoming the obstacles that may stand in the way of bringing a new child into your life (both for the sake of improving your marriage and to remain open to the possibility that God may want to increase your family).

12. Regularly look for opportunities to improve your marriage (read books, attend talks, go on retreats). Commit to learning to love more and better every day for the rest of your life. Plus, look for ways to be a witness to other couples about the secrets of living a Marriage Made for Heaven!

RESOURCE GUIDE

Whether you are looking for resources for continued enrichment or for assistance with a difficult marriage or a family or personal struggle, it is important to find competent help that is supportive of your faith journey. Here are some books, retreats, counseling services, websites, and other resources that can help.

FREE ADVICE! CALL THE POPCAKS ON AIR!

Fully Alive! with Dr. Greg and Lisa Popcak: **The Catholic Channel, Sirius 159 and XM 17.** A live, call-in advice program airing each weeknight across North America via satellite radio. Call 888-322-8465 for free advice from the Popcaks between the hours of 10:00 p.m. and Midnight Eastern (7:00–9:00 p.m. Pacific).

Heart, Mind, and Strength: Dr. Greg and Lisa Popcak host this live, call-in advice program airing each weekday on the Ave Maria Radio Network (or online at *AveMariaRadio.net*). Call 877-573-7825 for free advice from the Popcaks between noon and 1:00 p.m. Eastern (9:00 a.m.–10:00 a.m. Pacific).

Heart, Mind, and Strength Podcast: Listen to *Heart, Mind, and Strength* rebroadcasts via your Ipod or computer at *http://hmsradio.libsyn.com*.

NATIONAL COUNSELING RESOURCES AND REFERRALS

ExceptionalMarriages.com: Through the Pastoral Solutions Institute, Dr. Gregory Popcak and his associates provide professional telephone counseling services for Catholic couples, families, and individuals. Licensed counselors are faithful Catholics with comprehensive training in pastoral theology. The Institute also utilizes an advisory board of clergy, canon lawyers, and theologians to provide Catholic insights to complex issues of faith and morals.

CatholicTherapists.com: A national referral network of licensed therapists who support the church's teaching on marriage and the family.

MarriageFriendlyTherapists.com: A nonsectarian, national referral network of marriage therapists who are committed to preserving marriage.

WEBSITES

ExceptionalMarriages.com: **The Pastoral Solutions Institute.** A Catholic organization providing Catholic telecounseling, books, CDs an Internet ministry, and other resources to help Christians find faithful answers to difficult marriage, family, and personal problems.

CCLI.org: **The Couple to Couple League International.** A Catholic organization promoting Natural Family Planning.

ForYourMarriage.org: An Initiative of the U.S. Catholic Conference of Bishops supporting marriage and family life.

PopePaulVI.com: **The Pope Paul VI Center.** A faithful medical resource for women's health issues, treatment of infertility, and promotion of the Creighton model of Natural Family Planning.

TOBInstitute.org: **The Theology of the Body Institute.** Founded by Christopher West, this organization provides dynamic seminars, workshops, and media resources to help people live the Catholic vision of love and sexuality.

UnityRestored.com: A Catholic outreach to men and women who struggle with the use of pornography and/or sexual addiction. Information and resources are available as well as referrals for professional help.

RETREATS, SEMINARS, AND WORKSHOPS

Worldwide Marriage Encounter (*WWME.org*). A faith-based weekend experience that teaches a technique of loving communication to promote intimate and responsible relationships and offers community support for the sacramental lifestyle modeled by the presenters. Offered in English, Spanish, and Korean. Administrative Office: 909-863-9963. E-Mail: *office@wwme.org.*

Retrouvaille (*Retrouvaille.org*). A faith-based program for couples experiencing marital problems, it combines a weekend experience with a series of six to twelve postweekend sessions over three months. The main emphasis of the program is on communication in marriage between husband and wife. There is neither group sharing nor group discussion on the weekend. 800-470-2230.

Teams of Our Lady (*Teamsofourlady.org*). An international movement of Catholic married couples that promotes the spiritual growth of the couple and the family through a program of prayer and study. 903-535-7864. E-mail: *info@teamsofourlady.org*.

Couple Communication (*CoupleCommunication.com*). A secular program that helps couples learn eleven interpersonal skills for effective talking and listening, plus processes for better decision making, conflict resolution, and anger management. 800-328-5099 E-mail: *icp@comskills.com*.

PAIRS: Practical Application of Relationship Skills (*PAIRS.com*). A secular program that teaches practical skills for building and rebuilding great relationships. Effective with couples at any stage from premarital to deeply troubled. 888-724-7748. E-mail: *ePAIRS@aol.com*.

PREP: The Prevention and Relationship Enhancement Program (*PrepInc .com*.) Based on over twenty years of research, PREP is a secular program that teaches couples how to communicate effectively, work as a team, solve problems, manage conflict, and preserve and enhance love and commitment. Available in Spanish. 800-366-0166. E-mail: *Info@PREPinc.com*.

Relationship Enhancement (RE) Programs (*NIRE.org*). A secular program in which couples learn skills to increase mutual understanding and emotional responsiveness, resolve conflicts, establish more satisfying behavior patterns, and enhance relationships with children and co-workers. Participant's manual available in Spanish. 800-432-6454. E-mail: *niremd@nire.org*.

BOOKS FOR YOUR LIBRARY

General Marriage Improvement

For Better . . . FOREVER! A Catholic Guide to Lifelong Marriage by Gregory Popcak, Ph.D.

The Exceptional Seven Percent: Nine Secrets of the World's Happiest Couples by Gregory Popcak, Ph.D.

Feeling Good, Together by David Burns, M.D., Ph.D.

Take Back Your Marriage: Sticking Together in a World That Pulls Us Apart by William J. Doherty

Why Marriages Succeed or Fail: And How You Can Make Yours Last by John Gottman, Ph.D.

Ten Lessons to Transform Your Marriage: America's Love Lab Experts Share Their Strategies for Strengthening Your Relationship by John M. Gottman, Julie Schwartz Gottman, and Joan Declaire

Sexuality

Holy Sex! A Catholic Guide to Mind-Blowing, Toe-Curling, Infallible Loving by Gregory Popcak, Ph.D.

Good News about Sex and Marriage by Christopher West

The Theology of the Body for Beginners by Christopher West

CCL Home Study Course for Natural Family Planning, Couple to Couple League International (CCLI.org)

Fertility, Cycles, and Nutrition by Marylin Shannon

Getting Past the Affair: A Program to Help You Cope, Heal, and Move On by Douglas Snyder, Ph.D., Donald Baucom, Ph.D., and Kristina Gordon, Ph.D.

Intimacy after Infidelity: How to Rebuild and Affair-Proof Your Marriage by Steven Solomon, Ph.D., and Lorie Teagno, Ph.D.

Parenting

Parenting with Grace: The Catholic Parents' Guide for Raising (Almost) Perfect Kids by Gregory Popcak, Ph.D., and Lisa Popcak

The Intentional Family: Simple Rituals to Strengthen Family Ties by William J. Doherty, Ph.D.

How to Talk So Kids Will Listen and Listen So Kids will Talk by Adele Faber and Elaine Mazlish

Siblings without Rivalry by Adele Faber and Elaine Mazlish

The Catholic Home: Celebrations and Traditions for Holidays, Feast Days, and Everyday by Meredith Gould, Ph.D.

The Discipline Book by William Sears, M.D.

Parenting from the Inside Out by Daniel Seigel, M.D.

The Science of Parenting by Margot Sunderland, Ph.D.

Divorce Prevention

Between Two Worlds: The Inner Lives of Children of Divorce by Elizabeth Marquardt

The Unexpected Legacy of Divorce: A Twenty-five-Year Landmark Study by Judith S. Wallerstein, Ph.D.

Divorce Busting: A Step-by-Step Approach to Making Your Marriage Loving Again by Michele Weiner-Davis, M.S.W.

The Divorce Remedy: The Proven Seven-Step Program for Saving Your Marriage by Michele Weiner-Davis, M.S.W.

Address: 234 St. Joseph Dr., Steubenville, Ohio 43952   Appointment Line: 740-266-6461

Website: www.ExceptionalMarriages.com   E-mail: Counseling@ExceptionalMarriages.com

---

Marriage and family counseling agencies by their specific work of guidance and prevention offer valuable help in rediscovering the meaning of love and life, and in supporting every family in its mission as the "sanctuary of life."

Pope John Paul II, *The Gospel of Life*

Dear Friends,

I hope you've enjoyed *A Marriage Made for Heaven,* but everyone needs a little help from time to time. If you are struggling to apply your faith to your marriage, family, or personal and emotional problems, **The Pastoral Solutions Institute Tele-Counseling Services** can help.

For many people, phone consultations provide just the right mix of professionalism, privacy, and convenience. Because you make the call from the comfort of your own home, sessions are completely confidential.

Pastoral Solutions therapists are licensed counseling professionals who also have additional, comprehensive training in pastoral theology. We use a special clinical format that can help you begin to find solutions in our first session. You will end each phone contact with something new. A new technique, a new direction, more hope, greater resolve, and ultimately, a tailor-made resolution. And because we utilize an advisory board of theologians, canon lawyers, physicians, and clergy, we can offer the most faithful and effective solutions to the problems you face. A simple phone call could be your first step on a journey to a more rewarding, more fulfilling life.

It's time to make a change for the better. Call 740-266-6461 or send us an E-mail today (*Counseling@ExceptionalMarriages.com*). Let **Pastoral Solutions** help you make your world a better place to live.

May God bless you abundantly,

Gregory K. Popcak, Ph.D.
Executive Director
Pastoral Solutions Institute

A Marriage Made for Heaven

The Secrets of Heavenly Couplehood

This certificate is presented to

_____

For completion of twelve Heavenly Date Nights with your spouse.

A Special Message from your spouse:

_____

_____

_____

Summa Cum Laude

_____

Celebrant

_____

Spouse